Coach Benson's "Secret" Workouts

Coach Benson's "Secret" Workouts

Coachly Wisdom for Runners about Effort-based Training

Roy T. Benson

BEAUFORT BOOKS
NEW YORK, NEW YORK

Portions of this book previously appeared in *Running Journal* and *Running Times*.

Table C created by Larry Simpsosn & Associates; Ned Fredericks, Ph.D., Exeter Research, Inc.

Published in the United States by Beaufort Books, New York

Visit the author's Web site at *www.coachbenson.com*

ISBN 0-8253-0506-3

10 9 8 7 6 5 4 3 2 1

PRINTED IN THE UNITED STATES OF AMERICA

To my wife and best friend, Betty, for being

"the wind beneath my wings."

Only with her loyalty and tireless

support has any of my work been possible.

True sport is always a duel:
a duel with nature,
with one's own fear,
with one's own fatigue,
a duel in which body and mind are strengthened.

—Yevgeny Yevtushenko, Russian poet

CONTENTS

Acknowledgments ix
Introduction xi

PRINCIPLES OF EFFORT-BASED TRAINING
1. Individualizing Your Workout 3
2. Phase I: Endurance Training 17
3. Phase II: Stamina 35
4. Phase III: Economy 47
5. Phase IV: Speed 57
6. The True Middle Distances: 800 to 3,200 Meters 67

THE "HARD" SCIENCE OF INTERVAL TRAINING
7. Experiment 1: Intervals for Endurance 77
8. Experiment 2: Intervals for Stamina 83
9. Variables and Givens for Economy and Speed 91
10. Summing Up Interval Workouts 97

MARATHON TRAINING
11. Marathon Training 105

MORE COACHLY WISDOM
12. Heart Rate Monitor Tips 115
13. Biomechanics without Tears 119
14. Mental Training: It's an Effort 129

Appendix 133
Further Reading 149
About the Author 151

ACKNOWLEDGMENTS

It is only fitting that I acknowledge those who have made this book possible. Most importantly, I wish to thank my friend Larry Simpson, who first came to me to become a more competitive masters runner. Larry is a math whiz and part-time physiologist who has applied for a patent for a dedicated computer that uses a mathematical model to replace a human coach. I say this with tongue in cheek because we know that no dumb computer could ever replace a real coach, especially one as good-looking as me. Still, Mom didn't raise any idiots; I decided to keep a close eye on him by involving him in this project.

Since much of the material came from articles I had written for several running and fitness publications, a huge amount of editing was required in order to make everything flow together. Larry's job was to help organize my original material into something coherent and help pare it down into a simple little workbook that would concentrate solely on the design of workouts.

Special thanks to Amateur Physiologist of the First Order, Paul "Millimoles" Daniele, for all the outstanding work redesigning the pace and effort charts. His understanding of monitored training and his handiwork on the computer improved the charts immeasurably. Thanks also to Dave Martin, M.D., Ph.D., of Georgia State University. I have Doctor Dave's research and friendship to thank for providing data that validated what I had figured out through years of coaching: *optimized running performances require four different phases of training.*

And I don't want to forget fellow coach Jack Daniels, Ph.D., of Cortland State University. Most of Larry's data used to generate the original pace charts were mathematically modeled from the data reported in technical articles written by Jack. This same data was used by Amby Burfoot in an article he wrote for *Runner's World* several years ago, entitled "The Perfect Pace." Amby was one of the first to publish Jack Daniels' training pace table based on current 10k performances. Larry and I have expanded on their great work and, hopefully, by refining and adding, have improved it.

The folks at NIKE have allowed me to continue the study and refinement of the art of effort-based training. Their [techlab™ tools have enhanced the ability for all of us to fine-tune our training.

Without the assistance and guidance of editors, Carolyn Kolconay, Susan Hayes, Sheila McIntosh, and my friend and advisor, Sue Flaster, this book would still be a twinkle in my eye.

My modest contribution has been to link *pace* with *target heart rates* and tie this all together into the philosophy for individualizing training that I call effort-based training (EBT). Thanks also to all the many other coaches, runners, and friends who have supported my efforts over the years.

INTRODUCTION

COACHLY WISDOM

I probably make a better teacher than a coach. Scratch my tanned coach's hide and I'm sure that underneath you'd find a frustrated professor. In fact, it's as important to me that my runners know why they're doing a workout as it is that they do it swiftly. So I've collected all my answers about "why" and made them my modest contribution to the ever-increasing body of Coachly Wisdom.

"Exercise is good medicine." That's the motto of the American College of Sports Medicine. Imagine that! Doctors are now becoming coaches. These days they prescribe workouts as easily as they write prescriptions for pills. And, since turnabout is fair play, many coaches like me are getting very close to practicing medicine. We have become exercise scientists of the first order since our graduate degrees in physiology have earned us certifications from ACSM as fitness instructors and exercise specialists. So, that's what this book is all about: advice about running that is as scientifically sound and medically safe as my studies and years of experience allow.

To run is simple. Just do what you've done ever since you were a little kid. Put one foot ahead of the other slightly faster than when you're walking. It's natural, easy and usually fun, as long as you don't go *too far* or *too fast, too soon.* In other words, if you don't behave like the typical adult-onset-athlete, you'll enjoy getting and staying fit.

To become a runner or a better one, however, isn't always that easy. It's just like learning to play tennis or golf; it's hard and complicated enough to merit hiring a pro to teach you how to do it right. Well, say "hi" to me, your new running pro. You just hired your own private coach, someone who will lead you not simply by example, but by knowledge, training, experience and wisdom. And because I've been coaching for so long, you now also have an artist as well as a scientist working for you. This is important because experience allows the practitioner to be confident enough to get creative when exceptions start to baffle the rule. In short, I know how to individualize and personalize your workouts. This book is not a recipe by a baker who uses a cookie cutter to make every gingerbread jogger or runner come out looking exactly the same. Who was it who said, "Vive la difference!?"

With the explosion of knowledge about the science of exercise since that day in the late 1960s when Dr. Robert Cade invented Gatorade at the University of Florida, the following disciplines have now become fully involved in the development of modern runners:

- biomechanics
- exercise physiology
- sports psychology
- biochemistry
- sports medicine
- exercise cardiology

Relax. This book doesn't have much of that hard stuff and you don't have to learn it. When it does, I'll distill it into easy-toswallow drams of Old Coachly Wisdom. After 46 years of being a runner myself, I know what you're experiencing. With 39 years of coaching runners, instructing joggers and teaching beginners, I know how to get you where you want to go. Having studied exercise physiology and all the other subjects listed above since 1969, when I started work on my master's degree, I promise you that I know how to get you there with the minimum risk to life and limb. In fact, you adults might even find yourself getting better looking, feeling younger, becoming smarter, getting richer and even living longer in the process. Indeed, if you stick with your exercise prescription and keep working out for the rest of your life, you might be the healthiest, oldest person to ever die. Hey, think about it. That's not a bad goal, especially when you consider the alternative.

My secrets are to make the workouts simple and keep them convenient. In fact, nothing ensures compliance better than convenience, and using heart rate monitors and speed and distance monitors make workouts convenient. But your workouts must be designed properly if you are to reach your goal. Different reasons for exercising require surprisingly different amounts of quantity and separate degrees of quality. This is true in order to develop just and only the correct level of fitness associated with your goal. In other words, to lose weight you don't have to train like the star Kenyan distance runner of the week. You don't want to get that skinny and rich, anyway. I just want you to be incredibly efficient and not spend a skosh (n.: from Japanese: a bit more than a tad) more time and effort than necessary.

Most importantly, your workouts must be based on your current level of fitness, not that of well-meaning friends who may invite you to keep them company or experts who encourage you to just do what they did. Your body is not like everybody else's so you should not work out like everybody else. You're unique! You deserve your own set of parameters to pace your jogging and running. And those parameters are determined by your goal. So take a look at the following reasons for working out. Do one or more apply to you?

1. staying young and good-looking
2. becoming a recreational runner
3. competing at peak potential

Okay, I admit that those may seem a bit oversimplified. However, as you'll soon see, they are legitimate. Each requires a specific level of effort that results in very specific adaptations known technically as conditioning responses. We coaches know it as getting in shape. Whatever it's called, rest assured that there are different kinds of "in-shape." Trust me not to fool you about something so serious.

PRINCIPLES OF EFFORT-BASED TRAINING

I

INDIVIDUALIZING YOUR WORKOUT

Coach Benson's "Secret" Workouts has only one goal: to teach runners and coaches, respectively, how to select appropriate workouts for any given day, at any given phase of training.

This book has only one foundation: the *hard* science of exercise physiology. I am not writing about the *soft* art of coaching. That's the poetic way of referring to how I apply the principles of science to each and every one of my different athletes each and every day. I'm a pretty good artist today, now that I have had thirty-nine years of experience as a coach and forty-six as a runner. Back when I was a rookie coach, had I had access to the scientific body of knowledge that is currently available, I could have spent a lot less time learning the artist's brush strokes. In short, this manual is my explanation of how to become an applied exercise physiologist who works with runners. Combine these lessons with a little experience and you too can practice both the art and science of coaching middle- and long-distance runners. When you do, you will be following a philosophy that I call "effort-based training."

Effort-based training (EBT) relies primarily on the science of the cardiac response to exercise. Thanks to the availability of telemetric heart rate monitors since the mid-1980s, I have been constantly refining my belief that working heart rates can be correlated with two other primary ways of measuring a runner's training and racing efforts: pace and perceived exertion. Rate of perceived exertion is a subjective way to tie together beats per minute and minutes per mile (*see* Table A, page 135 for the correlations chart).

Until runners could use heart rate monitors, they didn't stop in the middle of every workout every few minutes to count their pulses. Sure, they were only too eager to stop after each repeat of an interval workout for a pulse check. But that was obviously just to delay the inevitable resumption of the workout, to gain an extra bit of recovery time. Out on the roads during easy or tempo runs, forget it. The word "repeat," by the way, is used to refer to all the running aspects of an interval workout whether or not they are all of the same distance.

Heart monitors — and now pace and distance monitors — make my approach easy to practice. By now we must be into the fifth generation of telemetric (wireless) monitors. They're small, comfortable, waterproof, and user-friendly. Above all, they're now actually cheaper than some running shoes.

Wait! Don't stop reading. If you think this is only going to be about training with monitors, you're wrong.

You don't win a race by crossing the finish line with the lowest heart rate. Time still counts. So, thanks to research on pacing by Coach Jack Daniels, Ph.D., *pace per mile* is the major part of my philosophy of coaching. Therefore, I rely heavily today on the work by NIKE [Techlab™, which has married time, pace, and heart rate into one monitor. What we get is a realistic way to measure how hard a runner is working at paces that are intelligent for his current level of fitness. Then, when I tie everything together with the string of "perceived exertion," we have a commonsense way of measuring the strength of that correlation between effort and pace. In short, effort-based training = beats per minute + minutes per mile + perceived exertion.

TYPES OF WORKOUTS

As both a runner and coach, I used to find the challenge of selecting workouts overwhelmingly complicated. There are still a bewildering variety of choices. Hundreds of books and thousands of articles offer readers many different workouts. Few, however, answer the ultimate question: what exact workout would be of the absolute most benefit to me right here, right now, on this day?

Consider the possible variables that might constitute a single workout:

1. General type of workout
   a. long, slow distance
   b. steady-state
   c. anaerobic threshold
   d. fartlek (A Swedish sytem that means "speed play")
   e. interval training
2. Current phase of training: Phase I, II, III or IV
3. Duration of the training cycle: 7-, 10-, or 14-day
4. Total distance to be covered
5. Pace of the run
6. Effort of the run
7. Length and activity of the recovery interval
8. Development of endurance, stamina, economy, or speed

Complicating things further is the fact that there is no standard training language. Anyone who has ever expressed a written opinion has invented his or her own pet names for certain workouts, occasionally even giving new names to those few labels that have become universally classic.

Although this book can't impose a universal language on the

sport, it can teach you how to select the right workout, in a very user-friendly fashion.

How do coaches and runners really know if the workouts they pick will accomplish the particular conditioning goal that should be behind the design and execution of every single workout?

It seems to me, since nearly everyone readily acknowledges that each runner is different, we can also agree each runner's workout somehow must be different. Or, better yet, might it simply be that the same workout can be run differently by each runner. How?

My answer is to *design a workout according to each runner's level of ability and current level of fitness.* In short: *just vary the pace at which each runner does the same workout.*

For example, Mary just ran a 5,000-meter race in 18:18 while Bill finished in 21:11. In their next major interval workout, they both could do 12 × 400 meters with 200-meter jog to a 70 percent recovery interval, but Mary should be running considerably faster than Bill. Her 400s should be done in 1:24.8, while Bill should run each 400 in 1:37.7, assuming that they each are hoping to improve a little in their next race by working at an effort level of 95 percent.

How did I come up with those times, you ask. See Table B, page 136 in the appendix to locate their current 5k times in the first column from the left. Then note the training paces required in the 95 percent column of effort needed to achieve optimal improvement. Mary and Bill's differences excepted, the only thing that these two runners have in common is that they are *both working just as hard.*

These percentages of effort should not be confused with percentages of maximum heart rate, although they are related. See Table A, page 135 to note the difference between *percentage of effort and maximum heart rates* in columns two and three.

I've used this approach of matching effort with pace to coach middle- and long-distance runners since the first time I palpated a runner's carotid artery back during the 1970s glory days of the Florida Track Club in Gainesville. In my curiosity to find out what was really going on inside all those outstanding graduate and undergraduate runners at the University of Florida, I took to counting heart rates. Back then I was assured by my exercise physiology professor, Dr. Chris Zauner, that a runner's effort could best be measured by checking the rpms of his engine — his heart rate.

Heart rates, I also discovered, were a better way to individualize workouts. So, for the last thirty-three of my thirty-nine years as a coach at military, high school, university, club, and private levels, I have been trying to figure out the best way to calculate target heart rates as the basis for preparing and executing (EBT) workouts.

EBT is a simple system. I've empirically and scientifically developed a way to measure if a runner is working out at the correct pace. It not only uses time per distance as the unit of measurement, it also relates your heart rate and your *perception* of the effort to your running pace. Consequently your heart rate becomes the primary gauge by which you individualize and measure all workouts.

Effort, in this sense, is a numerical index expressed as a percentage of a fit person's 100% capacity for exertion, i.e., all-out, drop-dead-at-the-finish-line effort.

One way to explain EBT is to compare it to traditional methods of prescribing workouts. For example, it's Saturday and the traditional coach wants you to do a three-mile tempo run at your anaerobic threshold (AT) at 15 to 20 seconds per mile slower than your current 10k race pace. There are several things that could be wrong with this plan. You may not have an accurate estimate of your current 10k fitness because your latest races have been on really hilly, slow courses. You may be feeling bad (tired and/or hung over) this particular Saturday morning. The IRS may have just announced that your tax return was incorrect and you owe them more money. The weather or terrain may be out of the ordinary. All these factors and many others could affect the level of effort necessary to keep the traditional coach happy with the time you take to do the workout.

On the other hand, a coach who uses EBT would approach this situation differently. Say she wants her runner to go out and run for 15 to 20 minutes at 85 percent effort. This coach doesn't really care how much distance her runner covers during that time interval. Or, conversely, she is not that concerned about the elapsed time it takes to travel a given distance. She saves that kind of concern for races and time trials. This is training. The coach is merely concerned with the *level of effort* and *keeping it constant* during the time or distance of the run.

Think about it for a moment. In the traditional way of coaching, the stopwatch becomes the Almighty. It's a tick-tock mechanism that tells us whether or not the workout was done right, often leading to confusion about a lot of factors, including a runner's mental toughness. This traditional methodology ignores the fact that it is carefully orchestrated *effort* and *not time-per-unit-of-distance* that maximizes the body's adaptation process, while at the same time preventing injuries. Thanks to telemetric heart monitors and EBT, the tradition's changing.

So, let's see how we can now use the heart monitor as a tachometer to observe exactly how your engine is running.

INDIVIDUALIZING YOUR TARGET HEART RATES

Monitoring your heart rate is the best way to get precise feedback about what your body thinks about today's workout. To get constant, reliable feedback, you need to use a heart rate monitor. That's why I urge each of my runners to train with one. Then, all you need for successful workouts is a good set of target heart rates (THRs) that are your own, not your partners.

If your goal for the day's easy run is to recover at a 60 to 70 percent level of effort, in what range should you keep your heart rate, 134 to 148 beats per minute, or 121 to 135? At your current high level of fitness, the answer might be 121 to 138, but for your younger running partner, 134 to 148 might be appropriate.

One thing is certain, THRs are like salaries: raw numbers should not be compared. You have to know several facts before you can tell if you should run together, not with the same set of THRs, but at the same *percentage of effort*. Training effects at a given percentage of maximum effort are universal. Everyone training at 70 percent, for example, will have exactly the same training responses. Paces may be different, THRs may be different, but the benefits will be the same.

First, to use effort-based training effectively, you must know your maximum heart rate (MHR). You can identify this either by actual laboratory testing (the most accurate way) or by using the age-adjusted prediction axis (the right hand column) of the Target Heart Rate Calculator (Table C, page 137). But training at a percent of MHR alone does not account for an individual's changing level of fitness. In fact, it penalizes more fit runners whose hearts are stronger and work more efficiently, by making them run harder than they should.

To help you select your training heart rates more accurately without a lot of math, Ned Frederick, Larry Simpson, and I have designed a training heart rate calculator that takes your fitness level into account. This utilizes the great work on target heart rates done by the Finnish physiologist, M. L. Karvonen.

To use our calculator you just need to determine two things: one, your resting heart rate (RHR), which indicates your basic level of fitness, and two, your MHR, actual or predicted.

Your resting heart rate gives a good indication of your basic fitness level. The more well-conditioned your body, the stronger your heart muscles, and the greater the capacity of your heart's chambers. That means a lower-than-average resting heart rate. For example, the average resting heart rate for a sedentary person is in the rage of 60–80 bpm. However, an average chronically fit male runner might be more likely to have a resting heart rate in the low forties, and a chronically fit woman's rate might be well below fifty. So, fit people need credit for their condition. It's one of the major payoffs for all that hard work. And remember, lower heart rates make your hair last longer. It made mine last until I was twenty-six.

Determining your resting heart rate is easy: put on your monitor as soon as you wake up in the morning for several days in a row. Lie back for a few minutes to see how low you can get your reading. Average the readings and that's your resting heart rate (RHR).

How about your MHR? What is your drop-dead-from-exhaustion-at-the-finish line rate? There are two ways to determine it: (1) have it tested by a cardiologist or trained exercise technician, or (2) use your predicted maximum from a formula.

Although it can be expensive, the most accurate way to determine your individual MHR is to have it clinically tested by a specialist who knows how to administer a true *maximal* stress test on a treadmill. (Don't take the test on a bicycle ergometer.) This means that the specialist lets you (or rather *makes* you) stay on the treadmill until you absolutely can't keep up your pace anymore and are in danger of falling off. By this time, your heart rate should have leveled off and refused to go any higher despite your increasing state of exhaustion.

Another informal way of maxing out is in an actual running time trial supervised by a trained coach or exercise physiologist. Knowing your actual maximum rate will enable you to tailor your workouts to your physical condition as closely as possible. In this time of rampant hidden coronary artery disease, adults should not try any do-it-yourself time trials.

For as much as 15 to 20 percent of the population, MHRs may be above or below age-adjusted predictions by as much as 12 to 36 bpm. These lost souls may find that maximal treadmill stress testing may be worth the money it costs because incorrect MHRs will cause THRs to be set way too high or way too low. Naturally, the resulting workouts will then be run at completely inappropriate fast or slow paces. If you choose to be tested, be sure to have the tests done by trained professionals. The emergency room is not a desirable finish line.

For most people who don't have the money or time to get tested, using the predicted maximum heart rate approach will be more popular. Much recent research has shown that the old formula of 220 minus your age isn't that accurate for younger, older and chronically fit people. Our new version of the "no math" training heart rate calculator has been designed according to the latest research on the subject and the current recommendations of the American College of Sports Medicine.

HOW TO USE THE HEART RATE CALCULATOR

Using the training heart rate calculator is easy. Forget every formula you've ever seen or tried to memorize. They are all incorporated into the calculator.

The Target Heart Rate Calculator (Table C, page 137) makes the math part of determining your THRs very simple. It is a state-of-the-art work-of-science that leaves no room for doubt or argument. Just follow the instructions and you're in business.

For example, let's say that you have a RHR of 51 and a MHR of 195. You want to work out at 60 to 65 percent on a real easy rest and recovery day. Draw your line from 51 on the left to 195 on the right. It crosses the 60 and 65 percent intensity lines at 138 to 145 bpm. To train at 60 to 65 percent requires a pace fast enough to elevate your heart rate to at least 138, but slow enough so that you don't go over 145. Although you won't feel that it's easy to run that slow, it's easy to know your target heart rates.

I have also found quite a few young runners (ages 10 to 15) and a few adults who are way off the charts — sometimes as high as 250 bpm at maximum effort. Don't be reluctant to use such high MHRs as long as they are validated by running at the paces that correlate with these training heart rates.

Depending on the size and nerve structure of your heart, you may prove to be as much as 12 to 36 beats per minute above or below the average predicted by the chart. If so, it won't take you long to realize it when you start training in your THR zones.

To validate your predicted THRs use the following method. Go to a track or other measured route. Jog slowly to get your heart rate up to 60 to 65 percent for a mile or two. Carefully stay within that THR zone. Then compare your effort to the perceived exertions described in the fourth column of Table A, page 135. If your level of exertion generally matches that of the description, you have good estimate of your target heart rates. If not, your MHR prediction probably needs adjusting. To do so, use the following suggestions.

1. If you reached your 60 to 65 percent THR zone at frustratingly slower paces than the chart describes, you need to raise your predicted MHR by 12 beats per minute and repeat the test before making further adjustments, if needed.

2. If you had to run hard as hell to elevate your heart rate to the target numbers, you probably have a much lower than predicted MHR. Go ahead and lower the age-predicted numbers by 12 beats per minute and repeat the test. Make another 12 beat adjustment if necessary.

This painless way of validating your target heart rates is known as Coach Benson's Low-rent Minimal Stress Test. If you try it and like it, you can thank me by remembering me in your will.

The following chapters will give you precise THRs that will show you how hard, in slightly imprecise THR zones, your body ought to be working. This admission about imprecision is necessary because honesty becomes your coach. Especially one who is also an exercise physiologist and knows that, quite frankly, it is impossible to run a whole workout at exactly one single THR. Furthermore, all good scientists know that each runner's exact capacity for oxygen usage varies with levels of fitness, percentage of body fat, and from person to person. So, to cover the range of possible variations, we simply assign each runner a THR *zone* because of frequent exceptions we have to make about changing levels of fitness. You will soon see in the following discussion why we waffle more about MHRs and THRs than Bill Clinton did about Monica.

COMBINING PACE AND EFFORT WITH HEART RATES

Theoretically, a runner should base all of her training and racing on just target heart rates. Measure the effort. If it's too hard, slow down. If it's too easy, speed up. Realistically however, the best way to train and race is to match beats per minute with minutes per mile. Let me explain how Coach Benson's Effort Based Training Pace and Effort Chart for Distance Runners, Table B, page 136 will help translate THRs into real world workouts and races by supplying the paces that you should be running.

For example, if you are a 34:00 10k runner or a 16:23 5k, the charts will tell you that a 5:47 per mile pace should elicit an 85% effort. To personalize this, use the THR calculator to give you the exact number of beats per minute you find in the 85% column. Since 85% is generally considered to be close to your anaerobic threshold when you are racing fit, running 15 to 25 minutes at your THRs at close to a 5:47 pace will take you for a good tempo run.

On the pace and effort chart you will find effort ranges that relate your paces to your THRs. As you can see, it helps to know what kind of shape you are in when using the chart. You can do so by either running a race, or by simply doing a workout like the tempo run described above. Just run it on a track so you know for sure how fast you are running. At 85%, read to the left and find a prediction of how you will do in a race. That's one of your challenges. You have to assess your current fitness level in order to determine if your individualized workouts are appropriate. Then you're ready to start putting together a complete training program of plans and patterns.

HOW TO DESIGN YOUR TRAINING PROGRAM

A training program is made of several components, all of which, in my system intentionally have the same initials. The first part is an overall view of where you're going. This is called, rather obviously, a Training Plan. See Tables D, page 138 for a blank sample and Table E, page 139 for one that's been completed for a 5k runner. It's a calendar of weeks over several months that lists when you are committed to running a certain number of miles, a specific number of days, how far you need to go on your weekly long run, and, most importantly, the dates and distances of any races you will run.

The Training Plan is then broken down into four training phases that last for various numbers of weeks. Once that's determined, you can write a Training Pattern for all of the weeks in each phase. Patterns are your daily workouts planned down to minute details so you'll know how hard and how much to run (*see* Table F, pages 140–142 for the sample).

TRAINING PLANS

First, make a commitment! Write down your goal in ink.

Write it right at the bottom of the Training Plan and race schedule. To start your planning, make a copy of a blank Training Plan and race schedule from the appendix and make a calendar out of the worksheet like I did on the sample filled-in schedules in the appendix by writing in the dates of each week during your plan. You can download a full-size plan from my Web site *www.coachbenson.com.forms.* I prefer to start my weeks on Mondays, but use whatever day you want.

Next I blocked out how long my sample runners were going to spend in each phase of training. You will need to read the following chapters on each phase to see why I choose the numbers I did. However, just know that I'm writing out plans for a fairly good veteran runner whose goal is to break 15:00 for 5,000 meters or for an elite high school cross-country runner.

Once I had determined the ideal length of each training phase, I filled in the races to be run during Phase III. In our life-is-perfect sample, I made up a season of races that would be good for preparing a runner to race 5,000 meters. I was careful not to schedule too many races, preferring instead to keep our runner fresh and eager for competition.

Once the schedule was determined, I filled in the appropriate Saturday workouts between competitions. The way to select them will be explained in each of the chapters on the phases of training.

Next, I assigned the long runs to be done on Sunday of each week. You'll notice that I like to make the long run short on a day after a race.

To decide how many miles per week to run, I filled out the miles-per-week (M/WK) column using fairly conservative totals in an effort to aim for consistency of training, rather than risk injury by going for higher miles. My philosophy is that *frequent* but *moderate* workouts on a *consistent* basis are the *key to success.*

And finally, I made sure that our runner had adequate rest days by filling in the number of days per week that he is to train.

At this point, let me confess something to you: there is no magic way to know if you're filling out a Training Plan correctly. It simply requires using some judgment while keeping an open mind. You may need to come back and revise your plan if you find that it isn't working. This is known in the coaching trade as the "Finagle Factor." In short, be ready to be flexible.

THE FOUR PHASES OF TRAINING

Over these past thirty-nine years, I have identified four separate *levels* of fitness that an athlete must develop in order to reach peak performance. This leads to the obvious separation of training into different *phases*. Workouts in each phase then concentrate on developing, in pyramid fashion, one level of fitness upon another. Using the laboratory language of the physiologist in me, I call these four phases (I) endurance, (II) stamina, (III) economy, and (IV) speed. Or using the more familiar locker room language of a coach, I also refer to these four phases as: (I) getting into shape, (II) getting ready to race, (III) getting better while racing, and (IV) getting in peak shape.

It is important to pay close attention to your heart rate during training to make sure that it matches the level of effort associated with your particular phase.

2

PHASE I: ENDURANCE TRAINING

Before moving a single toe towards the door, you must understand why it's so important to stay within the percentages of effort assigned to this phase of training.

Your responsibility as an intelligent, responsible athlete or coach is to be sure that the right physiological adaptations take place before moving on to Phase II. To make these things happen, you must follow the program closely.

Endurance will be developed when these bodily changes have taken place:

1. Maximum oxygen uptake will begin to improve because the heart, lungs, and muscles have gotten better at absorbing, delivering, and burning lots of molecules of oxygen.
2. Muscles will have learned to take the path of least resistance, thereby improving efficiency. This means that the body will move in a fairly straight line using the least amount of energy possible.
3. Muscles will have learned how to metabolize fat more

efficiently and become, in the immortal words of *The Complete Fit or Fat Book* author Covert Bailey, "better butter burners."

4. Tendons, ligaments, joints, and bones have had the several weeks they need to become as strong as the muscles will become after just a few days of exercise.
5. Fast-twitch type-two muscle fibers have been converted to look and behave as much like slow-twitch muscle fibers as possible.
6. Flexibility, strength, and coordination will improve from the aerobic speedwork.
7. The fine art of being patient will develop by learning how to endure longer and longer runs.

During Phase I, our main focus is on *endurance*. For veteran runners just cranking up for another season, this phase must be started a minimum of six to eight weeks prior to the racing season. For adults just making the transition from being a fitness jogger to a racer (whom I call an adult-onset athlete), another four weeks is recommended.

Endurance is technically defined as the ability of muscles to repeat a movement over and over again at a submaximal workload for a prolonged period of time. How prolonged? That depends on you. You can develop one mile's worth or a marathon's worth of endurance — it's all a matter of proper training. When interpreting this definition to my runners, I like to say that endurance is *the ability to finish the chosen distance, no matter how much you slow down before you are forced to walk.*

During this phase you should not exceed 80% effort, even on certain days I call aerobic speed days. I know that the term "aerobic speed" sounds like an oxymoron, but I'm talking about itty-bitty bursts of speed for very short distances that don't take you over 80% effort. Although 80% is borderline anaerobic, it's considered easy running in my system because not much lactic acid has a chance to build up. More about this in a moment. Furthermore, you'll notice a lack of recommended paces per mile for any of these Phase I workouts. Since we have no idea of your level of fitness, the smartest to way to train is strictly based on effort, as measured by heart rate.

THE EASY DAYS

Three days a week (for example, Monday, Wednesday, and Friday), I want you jogging easily at a 65 to 75% effort only.

One day a week (usually Sunday) I want you to do a long run at only 60 to 75%. Enjoy the scenery and think about something relaxing. The distance covered should be no more than twice your average daily mileage. On those other two days (Tuesday and Thursday), we'll do that aerobic speedwork I referred to earlier.

THE HARD DAYS

In Phase I, Tuesday and Thursday are not really hard. They just give that impression because they are faster workouts. The speedwork, however, is devoted to the improvement of your biomechanics, not to the enhancement of your cardiorespiratory fitness.

Why do you need to do aerobic speedwork? Unfortunately, all the slow, easy jogging has some undesirable side affects on your biomechanics. Your quads, hamstrings, calves, and hip flexors tend to get weak and unbalanced and your quads, calves, hip flexors, adductors and hamstrings tend to get tight. To combat these poisonous side effects of slow running, you need the antidote of aerobic speedwork.

But hold on. Don't worry: I'm talking about gentle, aerobic speedwork here. I'm not talking about the killer intervals done at

90 to 95% effort during Phase III and the painful 95 to100% effort workouts of Phase IV. We'll get to those soon enough. These are user-friendly intervals capped at 80% effort. They're short, easy runs of 50 to 150 meters done strictly for your legs, not your lungs. Here's a comparison between aerobic and anaerobic intervals.

AEROBIC SPEED	ANAEROBIC SPEED
1. the most fun runners can have with clothes on	1. pain, torture, and agony even with clothes off
2. must be limited to no more than 20 seconds	2. doesn't even start until you've run hard for a least 30 seconds
3. is run with smooth, relaxed, fast strides	3. you must be tight, tense, and tying up at finish
4. is over and done before a "first wind" blows	4. not effective if you reach a "second wind"
5. should cover between just 50 and 100 meters	5. probably is best endured over the last 100 meters of a fast 400-meter
6. absolutely hates lactic acid	6. teaches lactic acid tolerance
7. is the featured workout of Phase I	7. is the featured workout of Phase IV, the peaking period
8. may be difficult to reach upper limit of 80% over such short distances. That's ok. Just don't exceed 80%	8. should be timed on a stop-watch because it's scary to see your heart rate so high on you monitor
9. doesn't need a long recovery jog, but at least wait until HR=70%	9. essential that you take a complete "holiday" between repeats until HR=<60%

Try these aerobic speed workouts in Phase I. Save the anaerobic speed workouts for Phases III and IV.

Aerobic Speed Workout Sample 1

Warm up first, then do:

1. Four laps of striding the straights, jogging the curves
2. Four laps of 15/45 stopwatch fartlek (stride for 15 seconds/jog for 45 seconds)
3. Four laps of heart rate fartlek (stride your heart rate up to 80%, jog it back down to 70%)

Strides are fast, but relaxed runs at a pace you could run for about 2:00.

Aerobic Speed Workout Sample 2

Warm up first, then run:

1. Six laps of 150-meter accelerators (jog fast for 50 meters, run easy for 50, run fast for 50). In other words, shift gears every 50 meters, noticeably increasing your speed, but without going so hard that you exceed 80% by the end of the end of the 150 meters. Take a 250-meter jog recovery after each acceleration.
2. Six laps of striding 50 meters/jogging 100 meters.

I promise you'll love doing aerobic speedwork simply because you get to run fast and then slow down before getting out of breath and tired. Thursday's workout, however, may require a bit of huffing and puffing because it involves hills. Check the pattern sheet at the end of this chapter for details. But, keep in mind that raising your heart rate to 80% when you are not used to running hills seems much more difficult than Saturday's steady-state run at the same 80% effort.

STEADY-STATE RUNS

What about Saturday? Isn't it one of the "hard" days? Well, yes. Saturday is the day you get to have some old-fashioned fun by going for a real run. Your target effort is 75 to 80% and should last for three to six miles, depending on your mileage needs for the week. Your pace should be about 45 to 30 seconds per mile faster than your Sunday long-run pace. However, let your heart be the guide by looking up the heart rate range in the training heart rate calculators in the appendix. Later, your Saturdays will be switched over to racing or doing threshold runs. This is a transitional workout that will allow you to make the switch to Phase II.

THE SCIENCE BEHIND PHASE I TRAINING

Although the list of physiological adaptations should have given you a pretty good understanding of what's happening to your body during Phase I, I believe it's important that you also know some of the more important biochemistry as well as a little more physiology.

With the likes of infrared spectroscopy, chromatography, paramagnetic analysis, electron micrographs, and x-ray diffractometers, scientists can actually see the physical characteristics of some of the body's larger chemicals. These include proteins and enzymes that play a major role in running. Most importantly, we know more about the roles of glycogen, glucose, adenosine triphosphate (ATP), and those powerhouses in the running muscles, mitochondria. It's an intricate and complex system that far exceeds any mortal human imagination. You're going to be tinkering with the way your body derives its fuel, adjusting the body's ability to store those fuels, and messing around with your body's fuel delivery network. Because you're going to enhance its fuel processing system, you need to know about the chemical side of eating your veggies, carbohydrates, and proteins. I've found that when my runners understand what a particular type of training is trying to accomplish with respect to the human body, they are less likely to make mistakes with their workouts. The time invested in reading the next few paragraphs will be time well spent. It may keep you from huffing and puffing when you could be cruising at a relaxed level of effort.

When we talk about *endurance* training in the context of 60 to 75% effort, we're talking about training that is going to adjust your fuel ratio of carbohydrate to fat. Both carbohydrates and fat are used to produce glucose for the ultimate catabolism into the real source of all muscle energy: ATP.

Comparing carbohydrates to fats as energy sources is like comparing kindling to logs for fire burning. It's a lot harder to burn the logs than the kindling. But once the logs start burning, they last a lot longer than the kindling. In other words, although the fat is harder to burn, it is the better energy source. Remember, you want to become "better butter burners." So how do you become better at burning this fat? You've got it — running long distances at that 60 to 75% effort. The reason you've got to run slow is because, like those logs in the fireplace, you need lots of oxygen to keep the fatty flames burning. Aerobic running means running with more oxygen.

You may be saying, "I understand how this will cause me to burn a higher ratio of fat to carbohydrate during my long, slow run, but how does the body make a more permanent adjustment?" The answer: fats have aerobic enzymes associated with them that assist in the catabolism process. Long, slow distance running also increases these fat-burning enzymes. It's part of the body's adaptation process. This means that once you get your aerobic mileage up to a certain level, the body will burn more fat, *even in its resting state.*

ADJUSTING YOUR ABILITY TO STORE FUEL

As most of us know, the body doesn't have any trouble storing fat. However, it's not the same for storing carbohydrates. When carbohydrates are reduced to glucose, it will convert a certain amount into a slightly different chemical structure, glycogen. What doesn't get stored or used immediately is converted into fat for long-term storage.

Here's another benefit of Phase I training: Running at 60 to 75% effort will increase the amount of glycogen stored in the muscles. This means more kindling for the fire, and unless you're emaciated (less than 6% body fat) you already have plenty of logs. You need lots of kindling because most of the energy needs for faster running still have to come from glycogen.

Although it's true some of this increased storage capacity is going to be more or less automatic from the increased enzyme activity that results from all this slow, easy running, the greatest gains in increased storage capacity for glycogen will come from the body's ability to adapt.

There are really three rules at work here:

1. Your body will adapt to gradual and progressive loads or work.
2. Your body does not merely adapt, but actually overcompensates.
3. Your body needs adequate rest in order to adapt.

With respect to rule one, you are going to gradually be increasing your mileage during Phase I training. This will place larger and larger demands on your glycogen stores.

Rules two and three say that your body will not only meet these demands but, given adequate time between the long runs, will overcompensate by storing more glycogen. This is why Phase I only allows the runner to take one long run per week — usually about twice the distance of your average daily mileage.

Each week must reflect a *gradual* buildup of mileage. You can't be jumping from a 20-mile week to a 40-mile week, for example. As you increase your average daily mileage, you are able to handle bigger and bigger long runs on the weekends. How far you continue with this process is both a function of time and your target endurance level, i.e., one mile, 5k, 10k, or marathon. However, if you increase this mileage too fast, the musculoskeletal system will be one of the first parts of your body to let you know what it thinks of this folly. The Injury Fairy will tap you on the shoulder and next thing you know, you will have strained a muscle. But not just your muscles are in danger of strains. Your other connective tissues, tendons, ligaments, as well as joints and bones will also be at risk of injury.

These body parts aren't supplied with nearly the same number of blood vessels that reach the muscles. As a result of poorer circulation, they need much more time than the muscles to adapt to the stresses of exercise. Have you ever heard that old chestnut: "Don't run too far, too fast, too soon?" You can bet it wasn't made up by an out-of-work orthopedic surgeon or podiatrist.

ADJUSTING YOUR FUEL DELIVERY NETWORK AND FUEL PROCESSING CAPABILITY

When you burn fuel in your car's carburetor, there's a carefully engineered balance of fuel and air. Car manufacturers often enhance this process by adding special fuel injectors, additional air intakes, and other goodies. It also helps performance if the car has high-octane gasoline being fed into it.

The human body's fuel delivery and processing system can also be enhanced. Through long, slow running, your blood becomes "high-octane." That is, the blood undergoes an increase in myoglobin. Myoglobin provides larger stores of oxygen in the working cells for use when circulatory oxygen is inadequate. And you already know how important it is to have plenty of oxygen for the fuel-burning process.

I wrote earlier of scientists' ability to see inside the runner's muscle cells. If you were to look in your leg's muscle cells, you would find some tiny egg-shaped organelles called mitochondria. These are the powerhouses of the muscle cells because they are the only place in which *aerobic* production of adenosine triphosphate (ATP) can take place. The other system — the *anaerobic* production — the one that causes that dreaded lactic acid — happens in a fluid area *outside* these powerhouses. As runners, you want to delay using this other system as long as possible. Long, slow running will increase the number and size of these powerhouses so that you can do just that. With more factories for the *aerobic* production of ATP, you can handle the larger production demands of longer distances and larger workloads without relying too heavily on your anaerobic systems.

Closely related to this process is the increased ability, resulting from the long, easy running of Phase I, to supply blood to the muscle cells. The body accomplishes this by growing more capillaries to feed the muscle cells. This is an important issue since your blood carries oxygen and is the medium by which the muscle cells cleanse themselves of unwanted chemical byproducts — carbon dioxide and lactic acid. The larger the network of these capillaries, the more efficiently it can carry out these tasks.

IMPROVING YOUR HEART AND LUNGS

It's a myth that running increases lung capacity. However, running does strengthen your diaphragm and rib cage muscles. This means that you can move more air through your system and huff and puff longer without getting as tired. Also, your lungs become more efficient at transferring oxygen into the bloodstream.

Another muscle, the heart, also is strengthened. Over time your heart will become larger and it will be able to move larger volumes of blood with fewer beats. This becomes most obvious when you take your resting pulse. As you become more fit, your resting pulse slows. Some top athletes typically will have resting pulses between 35 and 40 beats per minute. The untrained person will usually have a resting pulse in the 60–80s. Something I like to show my runners is how lowering your resting pulse can lower the effort required to handle a given workload. You can see this yourself by taking my THR calculator and drawing a series of lines from different resting pulses to your maximum heart rate.

Although Phase I training will have the largest effect on the heart and your resting pulse, all the phases of training will contribute to the heart's overall strength.

IMPROVING LEG STRENGTH

During Phase I training, you will be developing leg strength to the degree that countless repetitions of one stride after another fatigues the working fibers and then causes fresh new fibers to be recruited to help out.

Like any type of weight training, overload must take place in order to stimulate the muscles to get stronger. As every weight lifter knows, there are two ways to build strength in the leg muscles: 1. *light* workload but lots of repetitions, or 2. *heavy* workload but *few* repetitions. Either method is equally effective. It's just a question of efficiency and safety that dictates which method we choose.

During Phase I, we are using the first method. Why? Because runners take between 4,500 to 5,000 foot strikes per hour when running slow enough to stay in the "easy" zone of 60–75% effort. The short stride employed during slow running represent lots of repeats of lifting our body weight just a little way off the ground.

Hence, light weight, but lots of repeats make runners stronger. Method two is employed during speed and hill work when the longer stride requires that runners lift their bodies higher into the air. As you can expect, overcoming more gravity adds more resistance to the "weight lifting" and makes the workout efficient because you get tired faster. And a lot stronger, too! This is why there is no such thing as "junk" miles. Every step you take counts. For now, I'm sure you would prefer running farther as opposed to running harder, so smile and enjoy the "easy" running of Phase I.

HOW FAR SHOULD A PERSON RUN DURING PHASE I?

The answer to this question depends on your training goals. Are you trying to get into shape for the mile, 5k, 10k, or marathon? Pick your poison. In addition, your weekly mileage will depend on what type of runner you are. The chart below shows my weekly mileage recommendations of 4 different categories. Review the definitions of each category to see where you would fit on the chart.

Consider yourself a *Beginner Runner* if you have been a Fitness Jogger for at least a year and want to start training with a racing goal in mind. A *Rookie Runner* is someone with a year of experience of running and racing. You'd define yourself as a *Veteran Runner* if you have been training and competing for 3 or 4 years. (A *Veteran Runner,* for example, preparing to compete over distances from a mile to ten kilometers, would want to work up to at least 40 miles per week minimum and around 70 miles per week maximum.) The fourth category is an *Elite Runner.* Obviously, this person should be a veteran athlete who trains and races to win and is willing to run as much as 70 to 90 miles per week in order to get that last ounce of improvement out of themselves.

Recommended Weekly Mileage

	Mile	5K	10K	Marathon
Beginner	15–25	20–30	25–35	50–60
Rookie	25–40	30–45	35–60	60–80
Veteran	40–55	45–60	50–70	80–100
Elite	55–70	60–75	70–90	100–140

Keep in mind that the mileage shown in the chart requires a gradual build-up. If you start experiencing sore knees or very tired legs, then, chances are that you are increasing your daily mileage too quickly. There is no exact science that I know of for determining how gradual you make the mileage build-up. Certainly, you would never want to double your mileage from one week to the next. Generally, a 10% increase in weekly mileage could be handled fairly easily. And as another general rule, you would never want your long run to be more than twice that of your average daily mileage.

PHASE I SUMMARY

Purpose: Aerobic conditioning to develop endurance, which is the capacity to finish the workout, no matter how much you slow down, without walking.

Conditioning Responses
Maximum oxygen uptake increases
Efficiency of movement improves
Metabolism of fat increases
Connective tissues strengthen
Fast-twitch II muscle recruitment increases

Facts and Figures
Mode: slow jogging and easy running
Frequency: six or seven times per week
Intensity: 60 to 80%
Duration: 20 to 90 minutes
Length of phase: 6 to 12 weeks

To help you get used to seeing the correlations between pace and heart rate, check Tables A, B, and C to see if your easy-run pace at your selected target heart rate makes sense when you see what type of race pace they predict. Remember that the common thread tying everything together is common sense. If the perception of effort and your pace don't correlate with the predicted race times, go back and check your selection of THRs. It may mean that you're an exception with a far lower or higher maximum heart rate than the average person.

CONCLUSION

Phase I is probably the most important phase of your training. The largest gains in oxygen power will come during this phase. You will be building a base upon which all the other phases of training must be supported. Without the physical and chemical gains of the body actually taking place by a proper and broad enough base of training, you cannot hope to respond positively to the higher intensity training of the phases that follow. There are no short-cuts. You should never exceed the 70 to 75% effort level except for the short 80% effort aerobic speed workouts designed to keep the muscles loose and flexible. Your Saturday steady-state run can also approach 80%, but keep the effort constant by slowing down the pace as you tire out near the end of the workout.

At the end of this phase, you should run a time trial or race to determine your level of fitness. All of the following workouts beginning in Phase II will be based on your current condition. Therefore, your workouts will be based on pace and its correlated target heart rates. For the sample runner, I assume that Phase I develops a 19:16 5k level of fitness. See the Pace and Effort Chart in Table B for the individual workout paces in the next phase. At the end of the next chapter we'll offer a pattern for Phase II training.

In this next phase, we'll maintain this aerobic base, as we will move our focus to hard days at 80 to 85% effort. These will be designed to delay the onslaught of lactic acid (the precursor of muscle lockup) during race conditions.

Please note that the following sample pattern is designed for a 5k runner.

WEEKLY TRAINING PATTERN FOR:

Favorite Reader

PHASE: I

FROM: *7/1/03 to 9/8/03*

EASY DAYS:

Mon. ■ Tues. ❑ Wed. ■ Thurs. ❑ Fri. ■ Sat. ❑ Sun. ❑

MILEAGE: Run anywhere from *0* to *8* miles per day, according to plan, at *65%* to *75%* effort. Your target heart rate range will be ____ up to ____ bpm.

These are slower runs for building either ENDURANCE and or RECOVERING from speedwork and races. Relax and enjoy them. Consider taking off one or two of these days or, if you must, jog easy within the mileage guidelines given above. This is also a good day for cross-training instead of running.

After running, stretch and run *6* to *8* strides for *10* to *15* seconds. These fast but easy runs will help to rebalance the biomechanics of your stride. Slow runs are bad for you, if they are all you run.

HARD DAYS:

A: INTERVALS

Mon. ❑ Tues. ■ Wed. ❑ Thurs. ❑ Fri. ❑ Sat. ❑ Sun. ❑

These are "speed" workouts for maintaining leg strength, flexibility and coordination.

First jog one to two miles stretch and run five strides for 15 seconds as a warm-up. Then…

Run **12** to **24** x **100 m** in **?** at **75%** to **80%** effort with a **100** meter jog recovery interval. Your THR will be ____ to ____ at the end of each repeat, and should be down to **70 %** by the end of the interval of recovery jog. Finish the workout with **2** sets of drills over **20** meters. (High Knees, Fanny Flickers, Skip Bounding, and Toe Walk.)

B: HARD AND HILLY HEART RATE FARTLEKS

Mon. ❑ Tues. ❑ Wed. ❑ Thurs. ■ Fri. ❑ Sat. ❑ Sun. ❑

MILEAGE: Run **4** to **7** total miles and include **8** to **12*** minutes of Hard and Hilly Heart Rate Fartleks at **75%** to **80%** effort. Your target heart rate will range from ____ up to ____ bmp.

After running, stretch.

***Total 8–12 minutes of uphill running on several hills with 80% effort as max. Recover between hills with jogging until heart rate is 70%.**

STEADY-STATE AND ANAEROBIC THRESHOLD DAYS:

Mon. ❑ Tues. ❑ Wed. ❑ Thurs. ❑ Fri. ❑ Sat. ■ Sun. ❑

These workouts are exquisitely tailored to build up your stamina without tearing you down the slightest bit. They are in the immortal words of my high school biology teacher, Fred Cook, anabolic, not catabolic. You can look it up. And while you're at it, note very well that these workouts are a far cry from real interval workouts, so don't worry if they seem easier than you are used to doing. Just enjoy not having to bust it for a change. Start both the below workouts with a mile or two of easy warm-up running and then, boogie on down.

A: If You Are in Phase I or Marathon Training:

MILEAGE: Run anywhere from ***2*** to ***5*** steady-state miles, according to plan, at ***75%*** to ***80%*** effort. Your target heart rate range will be from ____ up to ____ bpm and your pace should be ____ to ____ mpm.

4. Long Runs:

Mon. ❑ Tues. ❑ Wed. ❑ Thurs. ❑ Fri. ❑ Sat. ❑ Sun. ■

These workouts have two purposes: to build endurance during Phase I and then to maintain it during the other phases. Thus, note well the changes in your THR when you switch phases.

MILEAGE: Run from ***5*** to ***14*** miles, according to plan, at ***60%*** to ***75%*** effort. Your target heart rate range will be from ____ up to ____ bpm and your pace should be _____ to _____ mpm.

Be sure to stretch really well and do four or five 15-second strides to get the kinks out and to rebalance your prime mover muscles.

Happy trails!

3

PHASE II: STAMINA

Here are the physical and mental adaptations you need to accomplish in this phase.

Your stamina will be developed when these bodily changes have taken place:

1. Your maximum oxygen uptake will make another nice improvement as your capillary system greatly expands in response to the introduction of anaerobic threshold workouts.
2. Your efficiency will continue to improve as your body learns how to decrease wasted movements. Be sure that your arms are not making a rotary motion from your upper body, and that you are not overstriding. It might be worth having the biomechanics of your stride analyzed by videotaping yourself. See Chapter 13 for more on this.
3. Your muscles will now start to learn how to deal with lactic acid.

4. You will start developing the speed endurance of your fast-twitch muscle fibers as you carry a faster pace for longer distances.
5. Your concentration will improve as the harder workouts encourage you to pay better attention to where and how you're going.

During Phase II, our main focus is on *stamina*. The ideal length of this phase is six weeks, but it could be shortened to just four weeks for veterans who have been through these phases before. Stamina is technically defined as the ability of your muscles to move your limbs through a specific range of motion at a given speed until that rate of turnover can't be maintained. When interpreting this definition for my runners, I like to say that stamina is *the ability to get to the finish line without running positive splits; in other words running slower and slower as the race progresses.*

I oftentimes refer to this phase of training as *getting ready to race.* The phrase is meant to create a little preseason anxiety by including the dreaded word *race*. During this phase, you should feel the urgent need to develop a higher level of conditioning whenever thoughts about upcoming races release a flock of butterflies in your stomach.

Stamina is best developed by adding anaerobic threshold (AT) workouts for four to six weeks before the race. Your anaerobic threshold is the physiological point at which your body stops using aerobic production of ATP *in* the mitochondria as its primary source of energy. It switches over to its anaerobic system in the fluid area *outside* the mitochondria to produce ATP. In plain locker room language, it's the edge of your huff and puff zone. It's a line that, once crossed, means rapid lactic acid accumulation. How rapid depends on how far over the line you go. With AT training we want to take you *right up to the line,* without venturing over it too much or too often.

I recommend two days a week of AT running at 80 to 85% of

maximum effort as the cornerstone of this phase. Usually, an effort at this level requires a pace that's about 15 to 20 seconds per mile slower than your expected 10-K race pace. In the following pattern, I have used the 19:16 5K level of fitness for our sample runner to determine the paces of the workouts. You'll notice however, that the number of repeat 1,600s is a variable to be determined when the runner can no longer maintain the required pace at the designated 85% level of effort.

For more on the design of interval workouts, see Chapters 7–10.

The AT runs should last for 15 to 20 minutes. They should be run as uninterrupted tempo runs for the entire duration, slowing down slightly in order to keep the level of effort constant at 85%.

As you prepare for 5k and 10-K racing, these are the workouts that help you develop a proper sense of race effort. If you're usually guilty of going too fast, this slightly slower practice pace will give you a better feel for the effort you should maintain throughout a race.

WHAT ARE THE PHYSIOLOGICAL BENEFITS?

The intensity of AT runs makes them uncomfortably hard but sustainable for 10 to 30 minutes. You are close enough to the upper threshold that you are beginning to accumulate some lactic acid, but you haven't ventured past the threshold where the accumulation is rapid enough to cause you to tie up and have to slow down. You will also continue to increase capillarization to the muscles.

The AT runs are run faster and farther than the aerobic speed workouts you were doing a couple of days a week during Phase I. By running faster, your range of motion will increase as you "jump" farther with each stride. This longer stride will also increase flexibility in your legs and hips and strengthen them, because more muscle fibers are recruited to lift your body higher and propel it further than in the slower steady state run featured in Phase I.

Conversations with my runners as they are making the transition from Phase I to Phase II usually go something like this: "Hey coach, we gotta talk. I jumped into a 5k this past weekend and couldn't hold race pace. My legs started tying up and I was really huffing and puffing after the first mile or so." This is to be expected if you start racing before you've really had time for Phase II to take effect. This runner is experiencing a lack of stamina.

During Phase I, we were recruiting fewer muscle fibers and the intensity level of the training was low enough that we weren't having to take our aerobic energy-producing system to its upper limits. In contrast, as we raise the intensity level of training a few times per week in Phase II training, we recruit more muscle fibers and test the upper limits of our aerobic system.

Returning to my example, this runner was probably putting out an effort somewhere in the neighborhood of 90 to 92% during the later stages of his first mile and a half. Without an incredible running economy, this put him well into the forbidden territory of Lactic Acid Land. Having this happen so early in a race was suicidal. A countdown clock started ticking. That internal time bomb, known as *muscle rigor mortis* was about go off. The runner had no choice but to slow down in order to make it to the finish line.

In a way, I'm glad when a runner experiences this form of humility at the outset of Phase II. It illuminates the purpose of Phase II clearly. Whereas during Phase I we were working diligently on building up the runner's maximum oxygen intake (VO_2 max), like putting money in the bank, we're now going to help him spend his savings wisely. At the same time, we are protecting his hard-earned savings by continuing to maintain the aerobic base.

HOW DOES PHASE II TRAINING IMPROVE A RUNNER'S THRESHOLD POINT?

In well-trained athletes, the anaerobic threshold point is usually reached within the range of 85 to 90+% of VO_2 max. Keep in mind that you are just now getting into shape, which means your threshold point isn't going to be that high. That's why, when you start running at anything over the 75 to 80% effort, you will experience some heavy huffing and puffing. Ideally, you would like to avoid that until you expend an effort in excess of 85 percent. In that manner, when racing the 5k at over 90% effort, you won't have ventured too far past the threshold point and lock up short of the finish line.

Threshold running is just one more way the body learns to adapt to specific workload. Since you are running close to a 10k race pace, you are teaching motor responses to more of the muscles actually used in racing than you were during Phase I. You are also beginning to deal with moderate levels of lactic acid.

These runs, particularly the type of tempo run that I recommend, help the body learn a rhythmic recruitment of muscle fibers and firing order of brain messages that get the body ready for racing.

THE HOW, WHEN, AND WHERE OF PHASE II TRAINING

The primary difference between Phases 1 and 2 is in the intensity of your workouts. The pattern stays the same: easy days on Monday, Wednesday, and Friday. In fact, they get easier because the work of building endurance is for the most part done. The objective is just to maintain your endurance. Your target zone of effort drops from 65–75% down to 65–70%. Look at the Table C again and reset your heart rate zone. That's the good news.

Now for the bad news: Tuesday and Saturday are harder. That's why those easy days must get easier. It will be easier to replenish your glycogen supplies by working more aerobically. At lower intensity levels your muscles can maintain that higher fat-burning ratio you worked on during Phase I. This saves much of that glycogen for your AT runs. This is important because the harder, slightly anaerobic workouts are going to require a much higher percent of glycogen as the major source of energy for the working muscles. Since the restoration process takes about one and one-half to two days of digesting carbohydrates, you must work lightly on the intervening days.

On Tuesday, instead of those fun little aerobic interval runs, you need to substitute long repeats of 800s, 1,200s and 1,600s. A sample workout would be to warm up and then:

1 × 800 meters at 85% effort with a jog interval until the heart rate equals 70% effort or lower
1 × 1200 meters at same criteria as above
1 × one mile at same criteria as above
1 × 1200 meters
jog one mile to warm down

Saturday's change will be a slight increase from 75–80 %, up to 85% for a run of 15 to 20 minutes. This is a true anaerobic threshold run in its finest sense. Although you will find that it takes a fairly fast pace to get the effort up to the required 85%, the workout isn't a killer because it's over relatively soon. Furthermore, since the real secret is keeping the effort at exactly 85%, you will find yourself slowing the pace down more and more as the run progresses to the end. Of course, to be sophisticated enough to be able to do so requires you to constantly measure your heart rate. Since you probably can't do that and run too, *you need to wear a good heart monitor.*

The remaining days of Phase II training stay the same as Phase I. Thursday is still a day devoted to legs, not lungs. Go out and gambol around like a spring colt as you stretch your legs. Run some aerobic speed in bursts not lasting more than 20 or 30 seconds each. Avoid running hard or long enough to make yourself huff and puff. Stay aerobic and keep the workout moderate enough to recover by Saturday.

Your long run on Sunday is the same as it was during Phase I. Just get out there and grind out the mileage.

I have answered the *how* and *when*, now for the *where*. Because of the closeness we are trying to establish with your anaerobic threshold, we need to have tight control over your heart rate. You can do this in part by watching your heart rate via a good heart monitor, but you will also need to have a constantly controlled workload. Hilly terrain won't work because there is too much variability of workload. You must run on either flat streets or trails, or go to a track. Sorry. You can enjoy scenery on all the other days, but AT running takes total concentration and control.

Now take a look at that familiar Pace and Effort Chart and take note of the 85% effort column for Phase II training. Line up the time you got from your first race or time trial, and voilà, there are the paces for your various Phase II workouts. Kind of neat, isn't it? You now know how fast you, not your teammates or training partners, need to run at the Coachly Correct Efforts. Keep smiling. PR's are closer than you think.

PHASE II SUMMARY

Purpose: Anaerobic conditioning, which is getting ready to race by developing stamina, the ability to maintain race pace.

Conditioning Responses
Maximum oxygen uptake increases
Efficiency and movement improves
Adaptation to lactic acid begins
Concentration improves Strength, flexibility, and coordination improve

Facts and Figures
Mode: jog on easy days; run at 15 to 20 seconds per mile slower than race pace on hard days
Frequency: hard days: two or three times per week
Intensity ranges from 65 to 85%
Duration: 20 to 90 minutes Length of phase: 6 to 12 weeks

CONCLUSIONS

We're getting you ready to race with this phase of training. You're going to be able to do a decent job of holding race pace. However, you'll be chompin' at the bit for some speedwork toward the end of this phase. You'll not be all that comfortable with the start of the race when everyone is semi-sprinting to establish pace and position. You may find it hard to handle surges. Downhill running may not feel that great either. Most of all, you're going to have a bit of discomfort in terms of how you are able to deal with the build-up of lactic acid. All this is why we have a Phase III of training. It will be your first real introduction into speed work. We're going to teach your body how to deal with mean ol' lactic acid.

Please note that the following sample pattern is designed for the 5k runner who has improved his fitness level from 19:16 at the end of Phase I to 18:47 at the end of this phase.

WEEKLY TRAINING PATTERN FOR:

Favorite Reader

PHASE: 11

FROM: *9/9/03 to 10/20/03*

EASY DAYS:

Mon. ■ Tues. ❑ Wed. ■ Thurs. ❑ Fri. ■ Sat. ❑ Sun. ❑

MILEAGE: Run anywhere from *0* to *8* miles per day, according to plan, at *65%* to *70%* effort. Your target heart rate range will be ____ up to ____ bpm.

These are slower runs for building either ENDURANCE and or RECOVERING from speedwork and races. Relax and enjoy them. Consider taking off one or two of these days or, if you must, jog easy within the mileage guidelines given above. This is also a good day for cross-training instead of running.

After running, stretch and run *6* to *8* strides for *10* to *15* seconds. These fast but easy runs will help to rebalance the biomechanics of your stride. Slow runs are bad for you, if they are all you run.

HARD DAYS:

A: INTERVALS

Mon. ❑ Tues. ■ Wed. ❑ Thurs. ❑ Fri. ❑ Sat. ❑ Sun. ❑

These are "speed" workouts for enhancing leg strength, flexibility and coordination.

First jog one to two miles stretch and run five strides for 15 seconds as a warm-up. Then...

Run _?_ to _?_ X _1,600 m_ in _6:46_ at _80%_ to _85%_ effort with a _400_ meter jog recovery interval. Your THR will be ____ to ____ at the end of each repeat, and should be down to _70 %_ by the end of the interval of recovery jog. Finish the workout with _2_ sets of drills over _20_ meters. (High Knees, Fanny Flickers, Skip Bounding, and Toe Walk.)

B: Hard and Hilly Heart Rate Fartleks

Mon. ❑ Tues. ❑ Wed. ❑ Thurs. ■ Fri. ❑ Sat. ❑ Sun. ❑

MILEAGE: Run _4_ to _6_ total miles and include _8_ to _12_ minutes of Hard and Hilly Heart Rate Fartleks at _80%_ to _85%_ effort. Your target heart rate will range from ____ up to ____ bmp.

After running, stretch.

Same hill routine as Phase I

Steady-state and Anaerobic Threshold Days:

Mon. ❑ Tues. ❑ Wed. ❑ Thurs. ❑ Fri. ❑ Sat. ■ Sun. ❑

These workouts are exquisitely tailored to build up your stamina without tearing you down the slightest bit. They are in the immortal words of my high school biology teacher, Fred Cook, anabolic, not catabolic. You can look it up. And while you're at it, note very well that these workouts are a far cry from real interval workouts, so don't worry if they seem easier than you are used to doing. Just enjoy not having to bust it for a change. Start both the below workouts with a mile or two of easy warm-up running and then, boogie on down.

A: If You Are in Phase I or Marathon Training:

MILEAGE: Run anywhere from _ to _steady-state miles, according to plan, at __% to __% effort. Your target heart rate range will be from _______ up to _______ bpm and your pace should be ____ to ____ mpm.

B: If You Are in Phases II, III, or IV:

MILEAGE: Run anywhere from *4* to *8* miles, according to plan, and include *2* to 4_ miles/ minutes at *80%* to *85%* effort. Your target heart rate range will be from _____ up to _____ bpm and your pace should be *7:04* to *6:46* mpm.

Jog at least one minute to cool down and stretch.

4. Long Runs:

Mon. ❑ Tues. ❑ Wed. ❑ Thurs. ❑ Fri. ❑ Sat. ❑ Sun. ■

These workouts have two purposes: to build endurance during Phase I and then to maintain it during the other phases. Thus, note well the changes in your THR when you switch phases.

MILEAGE: Run from *8* to *12* miles, according to plan, at *60%* to *75%* effort. Your target heart rate range will be from ____ up to ____ bpm and your pace should be *8:39* to *7:24* mpm.

Be sure to stretch really well and do four or five 15-second strides to get the kinks out and to rebalance your prime mover muscles.

Happy trails!

4

PHASE III: ECONOMY

Here's what your body and head will have to achieve in order to make you a better racer:

1. A final increase in your maximum oxygen uptake, especially because the workouts make you huff and puff hard enough to condition your respiratory muscles (the intercostal and diaphragm particularly) really well.
2. Another increase in the size of the capillary bed due to the sizable buildup of lactic acid you'll experience during your speed workouts.
3. Improved flexibility as your stride lengthens during the fast interval workouts.
4. Greater strength in the working muscles as the faster paces make your legs push you further through the air, creating longer strides.
5. Better coordination between your mind, nerves and muscles as greater numbers of muscle fibers become involved.

6. Better concentration on the task at hand as your mind seeks the shortest path and quickest way to get these painful repeats over with.
7. Increased levels of human growth hormone contributed from the pituitary gland.
8. A probable decrease in libido due to the stress of heavy training.

During Phase III, the focus is on economy. This phase stretches over the many weeks that make up just about all of one's season of competition. For high school and college runners, that usually means eight to 12 weeks. For road runners following a careful plan of assault on personal records and championships, this phase should be limited to only two to three months to avoid getting stale or peaking out prematurely. The combination of training fairly hard and racing frequently is a potent one and can flatten even the strongest runners in a hurry.

My applied definition of economy is the effort required to run at a particular race pace. Thus, if you are an inefficient runner, one who wastes lots of energy because of bad biomechanics, your economy will be poor and your effort will be great. But, even if you are an efficient runner, if you're in lousy shape and trying to run fast, your economy will be lousy and effort great. In both cases it's because you are running harder than you should. Your undertrained muscle fibers will have to keep recruiting more and more additional fibers in order to sustain the pace you're trying to keep. The higher the number of fibers involved, the greater the demands for energy and oxygen. This will be very uneconomical, and the spectacle you make of yourself as you "run out of gas" (and O_2) isn't very pretty. It's the same for high-horsepower car engines delivering more rpms at speeds way over 65 mph. In both examples, there is a loss of economy as neither oxygen, glycogen nor gasoline are spared. So, it's time for some high octane, speed work!

Let's look at two runners with the exact same ability but who are not in the same shape. Both run a 6:00 pace in a 10-K. The runner who is in better shape from more economy training at a 5:00 pace will be running with less effort and using less oxygen and energy. That runner is more economical. However, if his form is not as efficient, that advantage could be lost. If the other runner, although not as well conditioned, is more efficient, there could be a tie at the finish line.

The moral of the story is that distance runners can't rely on their slow-twitch fibers alone to carry this race pace load. We need to be able to recruit some of the fast-twitch fibers to help out. Fiber recruitment and conditioning is learned through training. Phase III training will provide the right balance between slow- and fast-twitch fiber recruitment to do the job most economically.

Another component of effort is the muscle fiber's ability to continue contracting in spite of high levels of lactic acid caused by insufficient oxygen during ATP production. This is exactly the situation during racing. Phase III training will bring improvement both psychologically and chemically. Psychologically, you will learn that no matter how bad you feel, you won't die, and that you will recover and feel good again shortly after the run is over. Chemically, you will be improving your body's buffering capabilities — its ability to neutralize lactic acid. This will, in effect, give your muscle fibers more staying power at race pace.

HOW IS THIS PHASE DIFFERENT FROM THE PREVIOUS PHASES?

If you are like most runners, you couldn't resist the temptation of racing during Phase II of your training. Phase II involved getting you used to running faster than Phase I, but you still weren't into the big leagues yet. Phase II was teaching your body to delay the onslaught of lactic acid. Now comes the time to deal with reality.

In races, you not only take your body up to threshold, you go beyond it. Phase III teaches your body how to cope with Lactic Acid Land.

Phase III begins laying the groundwork for developing speed. Working on your speed is simple, but not easy. Basically, you have to practice running faster. This will mean only a slight change in your training pattern because only your hard days (i.e., Tuesdays and Thursdays) will be different. The recovery days of Monday, Wednesday, and Friday should still be easy workouts of ambling along at 60–70% of maximum, basically as slowly as you can stand to go. Remember that the purpose here is to get your legs' supply of energy (your muscle glycogen) back. Restoring the glycogen levels requires from one and one-half to two days after a race or a hard workout. If you don't like to run seven days a week, these are the days to take off completely. Go for a walk or do some light cross-training in the pool or on a bike, but take it easy. No huffing and puffing.

Rest assured that gold medals are usually lost on the recovery days! This is when easy workouts degenerate into hard ones because of a macho disdain for appearing to wimp out in public. If you can't stand being mistaken for a jogger, hiding inside on your easy days may be your wisest course to avoid overtraining. Your hard workout day of the week should be Tuesday. This is the day for speedwork, running some hard intervals on the track.

Before reading further, please look ahead at the section on Interval Training. It will save you much pain, torture, and agony if you can learn the wisdom of "Givens and Variables." Then take another look at the appropriate P&E chart at the 95% column. This is the column that gives your 400-meter interval workout pace. By now you should have a pretty accurate idea how fast you can run your chosen distance. Use this information to determine your pace. Don't pick a time based on what you want to run. Stick with the line under what you have run.

Let me repeat that this is a good time to look ahead. I strongly recommend you study chapters 7–10 on how to structure interval training in order to get the optimum benefits from your training. Your workouts should always be based on your most recent performance level, not your goal times. For the times you should run each workout is your focus is 5k–10k distances, see Table B. For track runners, 800m-5,000m distances, see Tables G1 through G3.

In my sample workout, each repeat of your interval workout will be 400 meters long, that is, one lap around the track. You will do this at the pace indicated in the pace chart. After each fast lap, you will jog a very slow half-lap to get your wind back and your heart rate down to 65%. Keep in mind that the fast laps should feel like mini-races because they are designed to duplicate the stress you feel during a race. You will notice that the paces are slower than you could do for one or even several all-out laps. That's a little bit of a problem, because there is a tendency to try to run each 400-meter faster than recommended in the chart. Don't!

If you are a veteran runner and notice that these fitness-related paces are much slower than you're used to in interval workouts, you're on the brink of a great discovery: you've been doing the wrong kind of interval work. Hard work at this phase of training is not all-out sprint work. These one-lap runs should take only about 90 to 95% of your maximum effort capacity. Surprisingly, that's all the effort it takes to keep you improving from race to race during your season. Harder, all-out workouts in which you tie up and die as you come down the last 100 yards are completely inappropriate. Don't kill yourself in practice. Save it for the race! That's the place to be a hero.

HOW MANY INTERVALS SHOULD YOU DO?

If this is your first time attempting intervals, do between eight and 12 × 400 meters. Some veterans can handle 16 to 18. Here is where your recovery heart rate becomes a big factor. You should be able to recover to a heart rate that corresponds to about 65% effort. When you slow-jog that recovery 200 meters and find you can't recover to this heart rate, it's time to terminate the workout. You are either trying to do too many intervals or you are running too fast. Don't try to gut it out.

You are going to be racing — perhaps a lot — during this phase, so your schedule needs to be flexible. On the week of a race, two miles' worth of intervals is sometimes enough so you can still recover by Saturday's race. If you're not racing that week, then go ahead and run three miles of intervals and just be sure to take it very easy the next day.

As for the rest of the week, your other hard days are still Thursday and Saturday. Thursday you can include a mile or two (how much depends on whether or not you have a race on Saturday) of fartlek on a hilly course within your run for the day. Fartlek training involves changing the pace ranging from jogging to easy, short (10- to 20-second) "sprints." I put quotation marks around the word sprint to emphasize that these should not be full-speed dashes that leave you gasping. Just make them fast but smooth, relaxed runs at paces similar to your Tuesday workouts. As I like to say to my runners, "Think legs, not lungs."

Saturday is either a race day or an AT run day. If it's a day for the latter, during an easy run of several miles, include a segment of 15 to 20 minutes at the 85% AT effort level.

Now comes Sunday. This is still the same long run day. However, if you raced on Saturday, keep it to no more than half your usual distance. It should be more of a recovery run (60–70% effort) than an endurance run. Don't worry. You won't lose your endurance as long as you're getting in a regular long run on the non-race weekends.

PHASE III SUMMARY

Purpose: The aerobic capacity or competition season phase to develop economy, the percentage of total number of muscle fibers recruited to hold race pace.

Conditioning Responses
Maximum oxygen uptake peaks
Capillary beds expand
Flexibility improves
Strength improves
Coordination improves
Human growth hormone increases
Libido decreases

Facts and Figures
Mode: jog on easy days; run fast on hard days
Frequency: two or three times per week
Intensity: 90 to 95%
Duration: two or three miles of repeats
Length of phase: 8 to 16 weeks

CONCLUSIONS

During the final phase of training we will attempt to put the sharpest point on our peak as we can. We will make our greatest gains in establishing lactic acid tolerance and buffering ability. We will also make the greatest gains in establishing all the neuroresponses necessary for efficient fast-twitch fiber recruitment. The bottom line is: you're gonna go as fast as possible! It's time to peak. Road runners racing longer than 5k should not do Phase IV workouts. They are not necessary for events that are run at or just above anaerobic threshold.

Please note that the following sample pattern is designed for the 5k runner.

WEEKLY TRAINING PATTERN FOR:

Favorite Reader

PHASE: 1II

FROM: *10/21/03 to 11/17/03*

EASY DAYS:

Mon. ■ Tues. ❑ Wed. ■ Thurs. ❑ Fri. ■ Sat. ❑ Sun. ❑

MILEAGE: Run anywhere from *0* to *7* miles per day, according to plan, at *60%* to *65%* effort. Your target heart rate range will be ____ up to ____ bpm.

These are slower runs for building either ENDURANCE and or RECOVERING from speedwork and races. Relax and enjoy them. Consider taking off one or two of these days or, if you must, jog easy within the mileage guidelines given above. This is also a good day for cross-training instead of running.

After running, stretch and run *8* to *10* strides for *10* to *15* seconds. These fast but easy runs will help to rebalance the biomechanics of your stride. Slow runs are bad for you, if they are all you run.

HARD DAYS:

A: INTERVALS

Mon. ❑ Tues. ■ Wed. ❑ Thurs. ❑ Fri. ❑ Sat. ❑ Sun. ❑

These are "speed" workouts for enhancing leg strength, flexibility and coordination.

First jog one to two miles stretch and run five strides for 15

Run *12* to *16* x *400m* in *92–87 sec* at *?%* to *?%* effort with a *200* meter jog recovery interval. Your THR will be ___ to ___ at the end of each repeat, and should be down to *65%* by the end of the interval of recovery jog. Finish the workout with *2* sets of drills over *20* meters. (High Knees, Fanny Flickers, Skip Bounding, and Toe Walk.)

B: Hard and Hilly Heart Rate Fartleks

Mon. ❑ Tues. ❑ Wed. ❑ Thurs. ■ Fri. ❑ Sat. ❑ Sun. ❑

MILEAGE: Run *4* to *5* total miles and include *6* to *10* minutes of Hard and Hilly Heart Rate Fartleks at *85%* to *90%* effort. Your target heart rate will range from ___ up to ___ bmp.

After running, stretch.

Steady-state and Anaerobic Threshold Days:

Mon. ❑ Tues. ❑ Wed. ❑ Thurs. ❑ Fri. ❑ Sat. ■ Sun. ❑

If not racing

These workouts are exquisitely tailored to build up your stamina without tearing you down the slightest bit. They are in the immortal words of my high school biology teacher, Fred Cook, anabolic, not catabolic. You can look it up. And while you're at it, note very well that these workouts are a far cry from real interval workouts, so don't worry if they seem easier than you are used to doing. Just enjoy not having to bust it for a change. Start both the below workouts with a mile or two of easy warm-up running and then, boogie on down.

A: If You Are in Phase I or Marathon Training:

MILEAGE: Run anywhere from ___ to ___steady-state miles, according to plan, at __% to __% effort. Your target heart rate range will be from _____ up to _____ bpm and your pace should be ____ to ____ mpm.

B: If You Are in Phases II, III, or IV:

MILEAGE: Run anywhere from 4 to 6 miles, according to plan, and include 2 to 3 miles/ minutes at 85% to 90% effort. Your target heart rate range will be from ____ up to ____ bpm and your pace should be 6:36 to 6:08 mpm.

Jog at least one minute to cool down and stretch.

4. Long Runs:

Mon. ❑ Tues. ❑ Wed. ❑ Thurs. ❑ Fri. ❑ Sat. ❑ Sun. ■

These workouts have two purposes: to build endurance during Phase I and then to maintain it during the other phases. Thus, note well the changes in your THR when you switch phases.

MILEAGE: Run from 6 to 10 miles, according to plan, at 60% to 75% effort. Your target heart rate range will be from ____ up to ____ bpm and your pace should be 8:26 to 7:13 mpm.

Be sure to stretch really well and do four or five 15-second strides to get the kinks out and to rebalance your prime mover muscles.

Happy trails!

5

PHASE IV: SPEED

Remember that smart runners not only train intelligently, they know why they're doing each workout. Those who don't wind up paying me to do their thinking for them, and, like the chimp said when he climbed up into the counter and took a leak onto the cash register, "Folks, that can run into the money." I'm all for redistribution of the wealth (I charge a lot for coaching) but following my advice here can save you from having to seek expensive advice down the road.

The adaptations you seek in Phase IV are:

1. Improved lactic acid tolerance.
2. Increase in actual leg speed by maximizing your working muscle strength, by enhanced flexibility and by improved coordination. These factors may be summed up as "better biomechanics."
3. The ability to stay relaxed at ever faster racing speeds.
4. Greater economy from greater strength.
5. Return of lost libido.

6. Diminished appetite, which helps you get down to your ideal body fat level.

Ultimately, your speed will improve, allowing you to come to a peak just in time for that most important race of the season. Depending upon how well you built your aerobic base during Phase I, you can plan to spend as little as two weeks and perhaps as many as several weeks in Phase IV.

Speed is generally defined as your ability to "sprint like hell," but I usually modify that to "the ability to run much faster than race pace and still be relaxed."

If you did Phase III properly, then you were not trying to see how fast you could run the 400-meter. Phase III was really more of an introduction to speed, during which I primarily wanted to ease you into learning to run fast. I was more interested in building your running economy. Yes, those intervals were fast — a lot faster than the threshold runs of Phase II. But they weren't (or shouldn't have been) all-out sprints.

In contrast, the intervals of Phase IV will be run at a 95–100% effort. You are going to have to depend more on your stopwatch and your internal perceptions than the digital reading on your heart monitor to determine if you've reached a 95–100% effort. These repeats will be run for such short distances that your heart will not have time to catch up to your legs until the segment is over. Your heart monitor is designed to average several of your rates. That is, it takes several internal readings and averages them before it outputs them to the liquid crystal display. This only further impairs your ability to get an accurate heart rate reading during very short interval runs. Furthermore, your legs will have run up an oxygen debt faster than Congress adds to our national deficit. Since you will probably reach the end of the repeat before your circulatory system can catch on to what happened to your legs, your heart rate may, in fact, peak *after* you stop running. Distances of up to 150 meters usually fit this category. Once you stretch it out to 200 and up to 400 meters, you may actually tie up enough from lactic acid accumulation that your turnover rate will drop off significantly. Once again, your heart senses that you're slowing down and may drop below your maximum. In short, rely more on your stopwatch and the training paces recommended in the 100 percent column of Table B.

Phase IV intervals are often referred to as anaerobic overload intervals. I strongly recommend that adult road runners concentrating on 5 and 10ks never run these longer than 30 seconds. Elite masters, 800- and 1,500-meter, and younger runners competing in high school and college races will need to run up to 400 meters to get the full benefit of lactic acid tolerance training, but only a few very fast repeats need to be run to gain the benefits. Long rest intervals (up to ten minutes) of recovery should be taken between repeats in order to get your heart rate under 60%. Be sure to heed the suggestions at the bottom of the pace charts.

As a sample workout, start by doing 4 × 150 meters at the pace shown on the respective pace chart for your event. During this training session, purposefully throw yourself into oxygen debt. Give yourself the usual jogging rest of less than one and one-half minutes between each repeat. Four such repeats constitute a set. Between each set, there will be a recovery period. I usually have my runners jog at least 400 meters very slowly during this recovery period.

Now you are ready for the next set. This time run 6 × 100 meters at the pace shown on the chart. Jog 200 meters slowly enough to return your heart rate to 65% or lower between each repeat before stepping up to the line for the next 100 meters. Again, jog a 400-meter recovery following these six repeats.

Finally, run 8 × 50 meters at the suggested pace. Walk a 150-meter rest in between each. Finish the session with a one-mile warm down.

HOW ABOUT THE OTHER DAYS?

During this phase, you have three days of rest and recovery, or a light aerobic workout somewhere between 60 and 70% effort. I suggest Monday, Wednesday, and Friday. Because the hard days of Phase IV are so tough, you're going to need these easy days to get those muscles reloaded with glycogen. In this same vein, it is important to put your Sunday, or whatever day of the week you take your long run, in the category of recreational running, shortening it down to around an hour maximum the week before a race.

Saturday will continue to be either a race day or an anaerobic threshold day. If it's an AT run day, continue to keep it no faster than the 85% effort of Phase II.

On Thursday, run another interval workout of longer repeats at the 90–95% level of effort.

THE PHYSIOLOGICAL/PSYCHOLOGICAL BENEFITS

You are going to be improving your biomechanics by running full throttle. When you slow down to race pace, your legs will feel great. Submaximal paces will be considerably easier to maintain. And this won't just be subjective perception! The prolonged periods of high lactic acid levels will improve your body's ability to deal with acid through its adaptive buffering capabilities. During Phase III the rest between repeats and the more moderate speed levels did not force your body to fully learn this science. Phase IV achieves this buffering capability more completely.

All muscle fibers have tension-generating protein associated with them. During Phase IV training, a particular type of fast-twitch fiber increases its tension-generating capability as another form of adaptation. In locker room language, these muscles become stronger. You will feel bouncier — a definite difference.

Your running economy will continue to improve. Not only will the muscles get stronger and be able to do more work, more muscle fiber will be firing because of improved neuromuscular recruitment.

PUTTING IT ALL TOGETHER

The real key to proper peaking is taking a lot more rest between these high intensity workouts. A 60-year-old half-miler I coached would cut down from his Phase I mileage peak of 120 miles per week to around 15 for the couple weeks before the World Veteran's Championships. Another of my 60+ year-old runners would cut back from his pattern of four days per week to just three workouts per week for his taper. The week before Brendon Mahoney, my miler at Marist in 1999, ran his 4:04.7 mile, he ran only two hard workouts. The Sunday before his Saturday race, he ran a positive split mile (1:57/2:17) to learn to deal with lactic acid overload. Then on Wednesday, he ran 4 × 400 in 0:59, 0:58, 0:57, and 0:56 with as much time between each to recover as needed, usually three or four minutes. Tapering off from the slow easy recovery runs to no running at all on recovery days is guaranteed to put the "zippity" back into your "doo-dah."

At this point, I need to prepare you for the next section. It contains detailed information about interval workouts. It has the tools you'll need in form of pace and effort charts to make up your own workouts. Those workouts can then be based on the important principles of individualization covered earlier. Be sure to carefully study the logic behind interval training. It's the key to knowing if your workouts are successful.

PHASE IV SUMMARY

Purpose: The aerobic capacity or peaking phase in order to develop speed, that is, the capacity to sprint and stay relaxed.

Conditioning Responses
Relaxation at full speed improves
Leg speed peaks
Lactic acid tolerance peaks
Libido returns

Facts and Figures
Mode: jog on easy days; sprint and run at speed 105–120% faster than Phase III on hard days.
Frequency: one or two times per week
Intensity: 95–100%
Duration: one or two miles of repeats
Length of phase: 2 to 4 weeks

Please note that the following sample pattern is designed for the 5k runner.

WEEKLY TRAINING PATTERN FOR:

Favorite Reader

PHASE: IV

FROM: *11/18/03 to 12/2/03*

EASY DAYS:

Mon. ■ Tues. ❑ Wed. ■ Thurs. ❑ Fri. ■ Sat. ❑ Sun. ❑

MILEAGE: Run anywhere from *0* to *5* miles per day, according to plan, at *60%* to *65%* effort. Your target heart rate range will be ____ up to ____ bpm.

These are slower runs for building either ENDURANCE and or RECOVERING from speedwork and races. Relax and enjoy them. Consider taking off one or two of these days or, if you must, jog easy within the mileage guidelines given above. This is also a good day for cross-training instead of running.

After running, stretch and run *8* to *10* strides for *10* to *15* seconds. These fast but easy runs will help to rebalance the biomechanics of your stride. Slow runs are bad for you, if they are all you run.

HARD DAYS:

A: INTERVALS

Mon. ❑ Tues. ■ Wed. ❑ Thurs. ❑ Fri. ❑ Sat. ❑ Sun. ❑

These are fast workouts for building STAMINA and/or STRENGTH or SPEED.

First jog one to two miles stretch and run five strides for 15 seconds as a warm-up. Then…

Run *8* to *10* x *400m* in *84–77 sec* at *90%* to *95%* effort with a *?* meter jog recovery interval. Your THR will be ____ to ____ at the end of each repeat, and should be down to *60%* by the end of the interval of recovery jog. Finish the workout with *2* sets of drills over *20* meters. (High Knees, Fanny Flickers, Skip Bounding, and Toe Walk.)

B: Hard and Hilly Heart Rate Fartleks

Mon. ❑ Tues. ❑ Wed. ❑ Thurs. ■ Fri. ❑ Sat. ❑ Sun. ❑

MILEAGE: Run *3* to *4* total miles and include *4* to *6* minutes of Hard and Hilly Heart Rate Fartleks at *85%* to *95%* effort. Your target heart rate will range from ____ up to ____ bmp.

After running, stretch.
If not racing:

Steady-state and Anaerobic Threshold Days:

Mon. ❑ Tues. ❑ Wed. ❑ Thurs. ❑ Fri. ❑ Sat. ■ Sun. ❑

These workouts are exquisitely tailored to build up your stamina without tearing you down the slightest bit. They are in the immortal words of my high school biology teacher, Fred Cook, anabolic, not catabolic. You can look it up. And while you're at it, note very well that these workouts are a far cry from real interval workouts, so don't worry if they seem easier than you are used to doing. Just enjoy not having to bust it for a change. Start both the below workouts with a mile or two of easy warm-up running and then, boogie on down.

A: If You Are in Phase I or Marathon Training:

MILEAGE: Run anywhere from ___ to ___steady-state miles, according to plan, at _% to _% effort. Your target heart rate range will be from _____ up to _____ bpm and your pace should be ____ to ____ mpm.

B: If You Are in Phases II, III, or IV:

MILEAGE: Run anywhere from _3_ to _4_ miles, according to plan, and include _8_ to _10_ minutes at _90%_ effort. Your target heart rate range will be from _____ up to _____ bpm and your pace should be _6:00_ mpm.

Jog at least one minute to cool down and stretch.

4. Long Runs:

Mon. ❑ Tues. ❑ Wed. ❑ Thurs. ❑ Fri. ❑ Sat. ❑ Sun. ■

These workouts have two purposes: to build endurance during Phase I and then to maintain it during the other phases. Thus, note well the changes in your THR when you switch phases.

MILEAGE: Run from _6_ miles, according to plan, at _60%_ to _70%_ effort. Your target heart rate range will be from ______ up to ____ bpm and your pace should be _8:13_ to _7:23_ mpm.

Be sure to stretch really well and do four or five 15-second strides to get the kinks out and to rebalance your prime mover muscles.

Happy trails!

6

THE TRUE MIDDLE-DISTANCES: 800 METERS TO 3,200 METERS

Just in time for this new book, Paul Daniele and I have developed a pace and effort chart soley for track runners. Although Tables G1, 2, and 3 include the 5k, discussion here is confined to the metric cousins of the 800- through the 3,200-meters. But before we discuss how to use the charts, let me assure you that I appreciate the differences between these real middle-distance events and their longer cousins, the 5 and 10k. As a matter of fact, the half-mile (880 yards) was my favorite event as a runner. My PR was 1:53.4 and my best race was a fifth place at the National AAU Junior Championships back in 1963. Those modest results today, with $2.95, would barely get me a grande latté at Starbucks.

At any rate, some of my best coaching results have come with half-milers and milers, including a University of Florida two-mile relay team that ran 7:21.3 indoors in the Astrodome in the early 1970s. More recently, at Marist School in Atlanta, where I help coach the cross-country and track teams, Brendon Mahoney broke a 21-year-old 800-meter record at the 1999 Georgia state high school championships with a 1:50.1. Before the season was over, he set our school records of 1:49.8 and 4:04.78 for the full mile, which converts to about 4:03 for 1,600 meters. That time came in winning the National Scholastic Invitational meet as he beat Allen Webb, whose 4:06 set the national high school mile record for sophomores.

Here's how middle-distance runners can use Tables G1–G3. On the left side of the chart are columns titled 800 meters, mile, two-mile and 5k. By locating your current time under the heading for your primary event, just read to the right across the chart. Under the percent effort headings at the top of the pace columns, you will find the recommended times to run the workouts.

Because our chart is based on mathematical formulas extrapolated from data in Jack Daniels' book *Daniels' Running Formula,* it may appear that the comparative times from one column to the next do not match up very well. It may seem that our mile times predict faster 800-meter times than one would expect. For example, a 4:20 miler may not be able to run the 1:58 for 800 meters that we predict. If that seems to be the case, try the Horwill Four-Second/400 Rule to calculate what they might run for a neighboring shorter or longer distance. His formula suggests a 4:20 miler should be able to run 800m in 2:02. Frank Horwill, the brilliant British coach of world-class runners, developed his formula to determine how much a runner should slow down per lap in order to double his distance. For example, a 4:20 miler running at 65 seconds per lap, should be able to slow down to a 69 second pace and run two miles in 9:12. Or, 1:50 half-milers would predict that they could slow down from 55 seconds per lap to 59 to run the mile in about 3:56. His formula may work better with the elite runners' times at the top of our chart. For example, the 1:42 half miler on my chart should run 3:40 for the mile according to Horwill. I'm more of a Republican, thus my conservative prediction of 3:45. By the bottom of my chart, the slow-down factor is closer to 10 seconds per lap. By experience, I have found that beginner runners do indeed slow more than Horwill would predict. Welcome to the "art" of coaching.

The 800- and the 1,600-meter have special requirements because folks who are willing to endure that much anaerobic discomfort must have very high pain thresholds or be just a little bit crazy. Training for the 800/1,600 meter races requires more emphasis on speedwork than we have included so far in our Training Patterns. Now it's time to include workouts at the all-out, 100% effort level. I do, however, have a confession. The 100% effort I'm using here is not necessarily going to take a runner to 100% of maximum heart rate or maximum oxygen capacity because the repeats are usually done over such short distances that the heart rate doesn't have time to go that high. So the times in the 100% column are calculated at 120% of the pace in the 95% column as recommended in Dave Martin and Peter Coe's excellent book *Better Training for Distance Runners.*

Every discerning reader has noticed by now that the speeds of the 800s and 400s recommended in the 90–95% columns of the chart don't seem fast enough. Well, they're right. But only when it comes to the development of leg speed and lactic acid tolerance. However, if there is one secret I have learned over the years, it is the value of interval workouts at these seemingly suspect speeds at 90–95% effort. The key to making them effective, despite the recommendation in the economy section of interval training, is to wait for the heart rate to come down to 65% by simply keeping the interval really short. Start the next repeat with very little recovery even if the heart rate is still as high as 80-85%. On other days, workouts for these runners, who are going to run fast enough to spend much of their race in oxygen debt trying to keep their legs from tying up, can be done at the times recommended in the 100% column and even faster.

So, obviously, what we need here during the Phase III economy and Phase IV speed periods are three separate and distinct workouts each week with highly specific, different physiological and biomechanical objectives. One of these workouts, let's call it "A," should be based on the paces recommended in the 90% effort column. Since the primary purpose of this workout is to improve VO_2, a workout of 4 × 1200 is a good example. Although I like runners to total 3 miles of repeats, it really doesn't matter if the workout is a little short. Keep in mind that this workout should mirror the fatigue response of a race with heart rates not reaching upper target limits until the last one-third or one-quarter of the workout. Keep this in mind too: runners don't have to kill themselves to increase their maximum oxygen uptake. *They should not be dying down the home stretch on each repeat.* They need only to run fast enough to reach 90% effort. Their legs will love them for it since this workout is aimed more at the cardio-respiratory systems than at the neuro-muscular system.

A second critical ("B") workout can be done over shorter repeats at 95% effort. For this I like the old chestnut of 12 × 400 at 95% with a 100-meter jog interval to get the heart rate down to 75%. The pace is obviously faster but still not anywhere near race pace so again, the interval must be kept short. Since I often find that my runners like to "cheat" on these two workouts by running the first repeats much faster than I ask, I like to make a deal with them. If they stay on pace over the first two-thirds of the workout, I will let them run a "waterfall" over the last third. For example, on those last 4 × 400s, they can run each one a couple of seconds faster. By doing so they practice saving themselves for the kick at the end of their races, running faster and faster the closer they get to the end. Remember that nothing beats negative splits!

The third vital ("C") workout is the source of that old runners wive's tale: "Speed Kills." Well, it doesn't if you run it right. Developing your ability to fight off lactic acid buildup near the end of practice or a race, is the goal of workouts run at the paces recommended in the 100% column of this special middle-distance pace chart (Tables G1-G3). Those paces just happen to be calculated to be 120% faster than the times at 95 percent effort. We did so because the distances you will run are often too short to result in a full 100% maximum heart rate. Therefore, time trumps effort. To get to that stage of hurting is going to require running for at least 30 seconds, *but no longer than what we recommend in the discussion at the bottom of the chart.*

Since the objective is simply to run as fast as hell, the length of the repeat should obviously be kept very short. The best distances would be 100 to 300 meters, with 200 probably the ideal; one to two miles total of repeats should be the limit of the workout. The key is to do them at close to top speed and intensity, but with a very long, easy recovery interval up to the point of letting the runner "take a holiday." A good example of a "C" workout would be 8 × 200m in times from the 100% column with a "holiday" recovery.

The secret to these workouts is that the recovery period must border on that "holiday" length because you want to be positive that all lactic acid-causing oxygen debts have been repaid before you take off on another repeat. Keep in mind at all times that the objective of this workout is to work the legs, not the lungs.

You want to develop leg speed while relying on other workouts described above to develop the rest of your physiological capacities like oxygen uptake capacity and lactic acid tolerance. Real speedwork develops your strength, flexibility, and above all, coordination at top speed. Then, when you slow back down to race pace, you will feel relaxed and smooth, yet powerful. To see the differences in the four phases of training of middle-distance track runners, please review the following:

Phase I: No need to change anything here. The objective is to build up your aerobic capacity without losing your leg speed. The aerobic interval workouts will do that nicely, so just concentrate on getting in as much easy distance as you can in order to build your base as wide as possible.

Phase II: Again you can follow the basic pattern recommended in chapter 3. One small change would be to include six to eight 100-meter strides after Wednesday's workout just to maintain the leg speed you developed doing the aerobic intervals in Phase I.

Phase III: This would be the time to start following a Monday and Wednesday hard-day training pattern in order to get in at least two of the three recommended workouts. You could rotate the three workouts in the pattern over a three-week period as follows: Week one — A and B; week two — B and C; week three — C and A. Since you're now in the middle of the competitive season, don't forget the conditioning value of the weekly races. Assuming that you're running in meets on Saturdays, you're getting three butt-busters per week. Rest assured that you won't get out of shape on that kind of diet. You should, however, run 8 to 10 × 100-meter strides after each easy distance run on your recovery days.

Phase IV: To come to a championship or personal peak, forget about your maximum oxygen uptake workouts at 90% effort. Just use the 95 and 100% workouts. And forget about your long runs for endurance maintenance workouts of 60 to 70 percent effort. Just go for short runs while you taper your mileage down by taking off more days per week or by just going to the track and jogging a few miles to warm up for a short series of easy 50–75 meter strides on the grass. Try to run them at the pace indicated in the speed column of the pace chart. The second "hard" workout would be the leg speed workout of 50 to 100 sprints. An example would be 6 or 8 × 100 meters with a 300-meter jog between each one. Remember that a major component of speed is strength and that strength can be broken down into two components: 1) muscle fibers that have been conditioned through overload to become stronger and better able to lift you off the ground, and 2) muscle groups that have been totally replenished with supplies of glycogen, the rocket fuel needed to supply anaerobic effort.

Summary: We tend to overlook one training factor that can have a great impact on our racing readiness — consistency. All it really takes to perform up to our full potential is following a training program that offers *frequent* workouts at a *moderately* hard effort on a *consistent* basis. As many wise coaches have warned their runners, "The secret is that there are no secrets." To which I have to add, "Except in this book, which contains only *my* 'secret' workouts." However, if you try them, they should result in that most desired training goal: consistent days, weeks, and months of training without interuptions from injuries or illness.

At this point I need to prepare you for the next section. It contains detailed information about interval workouts. It has the tools you'll need in the form of pace and effort charts to make up your own workouts. Those workouts can then be based on the important principles of individualization covered earlier. Be sure to carefully study the logic behind interval training. It is the key to knowing if your workouts are successful.

THE "HARD" SCIENCE OF INTERVAL TRAINING

7

EXPERIMENT 1: INTERVALS FOR ENDURANCE

Let me ask you an important question: what are the components of an experiment? If you answered that an experiment is made up of givens and variables that allow you to test a theory, you obviously paid attention in your chemistry class. You learned that by controlling some givens, while allowing one part of the experiment to vary, a good scientist can measure changes and what causes them.

Well, guess what? Your training is nothing more than just a great big experiment. And, unless you know how to design the controls and the variables of your workouts, improvement can prove to be fairly elusive and highly unpredictable. So, fellow scientists, let's start by seeing what knowledge you brought with you to class.

Which of the following are the five variables of the experiment known as an interval workout?

1. distance to be repeated
2. number of repeats
3. phase of training
4. pace of repeats
5. effort of the repeats
6. time and activity of recovery period

Now just relax. You don't have to worry about answering any more questions. The pop quiz is over. From here on, I have the answers to your questions — and I mean every single one you could ever dream up — about the miracle-making workout known as *interval training*.

Oops, I take back that statement about no more questions. Here are a couple more: Why did Emil Zatopek run 50 × 400-meter repeats in the morning and then repeat that workout in the afternoon? No, he wasn't crazy. He ran over 30 miles per day because, in order to win the 5,000-meter, the 10,000-meter and the marathon in the Helsinki Olympics in 1952, he needed to maximize which one of the following components of fitness?

1. endurance.
2. stamina
3. economy
4. leg speed

Well, how did you do? Did you answer the question about the components of interval training by checking all but number three? And did you pick number one as your answer about the components of fitness? If not, go out and run 20 miles while reviewing everything you learned in PE 101 — Beginning Running. Then take the quiz again. Do this over and over until you get it right. No, I'm just kidding. This isn't football practice. Just keep reading.

After you read the two lists above, do you see the connection between interval training and developing the fitness to run peak performances? If not, rest assured that you can take your shape from below lousy as a rank beginner to the personal record shape of a champion without ever leaving the track. Just run appropriate interval workouts during the four phases of training that I detailed previously and you will take the required journey from the bottom to the top of the training triangle. As you go up, you'll develop, in order, those elements of a runner's fitness.

Yes, it's true. Interval workouts can develop every single component of a runner's fitness. For example, leg speed is improved on the track by running a few, short, very fast sprints with long periods of full recovery. Endurance, in the case of the immortal Zatopek, was created on a forest path as he ran comfortably, without timing himself, all those 400-meter repeats. His interval of recovery was, by the way, usually a 200-meter jog. Another of his favorite workouts was 20 × 200 meters and then 40 × 400 followed by 20 × 200. He recovered by jogging 200 meters between each of the 80 repeats. If you add up the distance covered in the workout, I'd guess your total will be around 25 miles.

Here's the point: I am going to show you how to use intervals properly within the context of modern training. In the process, you will learn to think like a scientist. You will realize that *every workout you run should have a stated objective before you start.* You will know which parts of your workouts are the givens. You will learn how to select the *variable* that will allow you to measure a certain component of your fitness so you will be doing the workout correctly. Although your pace may never reach missile speed, you will get fast and smart enough to become one of the proverbial scientists rocketing down the road.

If he were alive and training today, Emil Zatopek might not be running intervals to develop endurance. High volume, low intensity interval workouts like his famous forest repeats have been replaced by running, not endless repeats in the secrecy of a forest or the privacy of a track, but by easy, nonstop long runs on the roads, or trails, if you can find one long enough.

That development aside, let me show you the format for the classic experiment of intervals. It is the formula we coaches use when writing out what we want you to run:

Number *of repeats* × **distance** *to be repeated* in **time** at *percent of* **effort** with **interval** *of recovery*

When using that formula to conduct an experiment about fitness, one of the blanks is left unfilled and is therefore the variable.

Here's what Zatopek's workout would have looked like:

50 × *400 meters* in **??** at *70–80%* with *200-meter jog*

The givens were arbitrarily selected as dictated by the objective of the workout, in this case endurance. Zatopek wanted to cover lots of distance so he had to multiply his rather short repeats by a high number. He didn't time his 400s because he didn't care if he had to slow down in order to meet the high mileage objective of the workout.

Pace was thus the variable because it didn't matter if he could not maintain it. That fits my very own coachly definition of endurance, the ability to run from point A to point B, no matter how much you have to slow down, as long as you don't walk. Since Emil was apparently working on widening his aerobic base, I have editorially added the effort zone that I expect he was targeting. Assuming he was using his heart rate as a measurement of how hard he was working, he would have stayed within the 70–80% zone. This level of effort builds endurance while running paces ranging from easy up to steady-state.

With all that said, let me admit why today's runners would never use interval training to develop their endurance. It's too damn boring. These days, most runners simply go for a long, slow, continuous run on the roads or trails. A runner or the coach simply uses common sense to decide how many miles need to be run each week. These are then run each day in a nice aerobic fashion within the 60–80% effort zone. As you saw earlier, I have variations on that principle, but you can thank New Zealand's brilliant coach Arthur Lydiard for freeing you from endless interval workouts at the track. His philosophy was to train even half-milers like marathoners with 100 miles per week on roads and trails.

You locker room lawyers realize, of course, that the classic formula for an interval workout does not include effort zones. Being the modern coach and low-rent scientist that I am, I have added "percent effort" in order to better measure if a runner is going too fast or too slow for the stated objective of the workout. This has been made easy with the acceptance of heart rate monitors by so many runners. And, fellow scientists, remember that the more controls our experiment has, the more reliable our measurement of the variable.

8

EXPERIMENT 2: INTERVALS FOR STAMINA

Study the following formula for success and then identify who made it forever famous: 10 × 440 yards in 59 seconds with a two-minute jog interval.

Challenging workout wasn't it? But did you notice there doesn't seem to be a variable amongst the givens? Who was responsible for such a violation of the experimental model? Hint: he was, of all things, a researcher studying respiratory reactions to running. How ironic this appears at first glance because it was Dr. Roger Bannister's key workout. Read on in search of the elusive variable and let's see if the good doctor was a true scientist.

Dr. Bannister, as everyone who runs should know, was the first person in history to break the barrier of the 4:00 mile. He did so by training, almost exclusively, six days a week with interval workouts. After developing his endurance and an initial level of stamina during the cross-country season, he started his interval work with the goal of running 10 × 440 yards in less than 60 seconds per 440 with a 2:00 recovery interval. He assumed that when he could do that workout, he would be ready to run four sub-60 second 440s in a row in a race. Four days a week, Bannister would take a half hour from his busy medical studies to join the Paddington lunch bunch for interval workouts. Friday and Saturday training sessions consisted of more intervals at a different venue where Franz Stampfl, coach of his training partner Chris Brasher, would hold more of these strenuous stamina and speed workouts.

Starting in December of 1953, Bannister and his training mates at Paddington began the track phase of their training with their first 440 interval workout. They averaged 66 seconds per 440 for the 10 repeats while taking a 2:00 interval of jogging between 440s. Their goal was to bring the time down, little by little, week after week, until Bannister could do them all under 60 seconds. *Now* have you found the variable? In this case, it was time, or pace of the repeats, so he could be sure his stamina was adequate for the 4:00 mile.

Emil Zatopek, on the other hand, had simply wanted to build an endurance base of big kilometers. So his goal was just to complete his chosen workout of high volume at whatever pace he could manage. If he got slower the more he ran, it was okay as long as he finished the workout. Bannister felt he had enough endurance from running cross-country in the fall. Although his weekly mileage totals were absolutely puny compared to Zatopek's, he was able to win a 7.5 mile cross-country race off what he did run. So, Bannister's experiment on that first day of track work was simply to see how fast he could run the 10 × 440. Just like Zatopek, he picked a certain number of repeats, the distance to be repeated, and a particular rest interval calculated to allow enough recovery from his high-intensity efforts. The variable was time, or pace as we also call it. In this case, it was not only counted in seconds/440, it was also measured in weeks. At the start of this phase, it turned out that the best he could do was average 66 seconds for his quarter-mile (440 yard) repeats.

By April, Bannister had improved his stamina, but found himself stuck at 61 seconds per 440. Each workout, he tried harder. But 61 seconds was the best he could run. He concluded he was flat and close to becoming overtrained. To get over his staleness, he decided to go hiking in the Scottish Highlands with Brasher. It worked. After this four-day holiday, he came back to Paddington, nailed the workout by averaging 59 seconds per 440 and proclaimed that he was ready for his grand assault on the 4:00 barrier.

As you know, that succeeded, too. On May 6, 1954, he became the first person in history to run one mile under 4:00. His new world record was 3:59.4, thanks to the specificity of his interval training. And, thanks too, to a nice taper. Can you imagine taking off five whole days off before a race like he did for this one? He certainly had a lot of faith in freshness.

When comparing Bannister's meager daily mileage with the 40,000 meters run by Emil Zatopek, one wonders how two runners could have such wildly different approaches. The answer is, of course, that it depended on the *objective* of the workout, which in turn, depended on the distances of the goal races. Zatopek needed lots of endurance to finish all those kilometers. Bannister needed less endurance but more stamina to run his meager mile.

At this point, perhaps you are confused by all this switching around from yards to meters. Let me clarify the language of interval training, especially when it concerns the distances referred to in these different examples.

While the Europeans measure distance in meters and kilometers and we are still measuring distances by yards and miles, the difference between 400 meters and 440 yards, while barely discernible, is significant. For example, if you ran four laps around a 400-meter track and you wanted to know what your time would have been for the slightly longer one mile, you can simply add the 1.5 to 1.9 seconds it would take most of us to run the extra 30 feet.

That's right. The difference between 400 meters and 440 yards is just 7'6" longer for the yards.

Now, just in case you haven't been told, all the running tracks in the U.S. have been converted to 400 meters in an effort to make our records comparable to those set by the rest of the world. Today, Italians can compare their times for 800 meters with ours. But, of course, not a single American has any idea of how well our athletes are performing because we're not really sure how 100 yards compares to 100 meters, and so forth. Furthermore, our road races are stupidly run over 5,000 and 10,000 meters (5k and 10k races) while splits are intelligently offered at the mile marks. Talk about split personalities and paranoia. You'd think someone is out to get us.

Excuse, please, the tone of those comments, but the irrationality of the way we measure racing distances here in the good old U.S.A. is a sore point with your old coach. Why don't we just stop after three or six miles and say to hell with that extra, superfluous distance of 176 or 352 yards? Believe me, if I were king, we would. In fact, our brand new $450,000 Mondo track at Marist School is specially marked with a separate starting line for the mile run. It's 30 feet behind the standard finish line for the 400-meter lap. And every 7'6" up the track from the mile starting line has a hash mark indicating each 440-yard split needed to make it an even mile. We're not going to run 3:58.3 for 1600 meters and then have some propellerhead with a slide rule from USA Track & Field (USAT&F) tell us that the actual adjustment at 4:00 pace is 1.8 seconds. We're running the whole mile and then letting the Europeans figure out how fast we went through the 1,500 meters. That's not a typo. Not only are they too lazy to run a full quarter-mile per lap on their way to 1,600 meters, they have to have a 100-meter handicap before they even start running their so-called "metric mile." Metric mile? Baloney! How about the Magic Mile with its 4:00 challenge? Imagine Roger Bannister being proud to the first person to break 4:00 for the metric mile of 1,500 lousy meters. Until everything in America is converted to metric, I say, "Roger Bannister for King!" At least king of the milers.

Excuse that diatribe. Let me now ask, "Endurance and stamina: what's the difference?" Why does it matter? Well, those are questions that need to be raised as we study interval training, the running world's most important, yet mystifying, workouts. Like kids with the birds and the bees, everyone talks about it, but few understand what's really going on. Hence this attempt at making you a better beekeeper and to help you understand how you can get a better buzz from your workouts.

At this point, you have seen examples of workouts used by two of history's most successful practitioners of interval training. You saw how they selected the givens of their interval experiment by understanding the objectives of their workouts. They or their coaches knew how to train through the four phases of conditioning required to reach a peak ready to set personal records. Of course, in the cases of both Emil Zatopek and Roger Bannister, *those* PRs were also going to be Olympic and world records. But the training you do is still the same. It's just that your paces will probably be slower. Your efforts will be the same as theirs: as great on the hard days and as easy on the recovery days. That's the beauty of the universal response to the stresses of exercise. All of us will have, for example, the same getting-into-shape reaction to the easy, endurance building efforts from training within the 60– 80% effort zone. The runners with the most natural talent simply get their workouts over sooner than the rest of us. But that doesn't make them better than us. Just faster.

Unfortunately, the most common mistake made by both veteran and rookie runners is using someone else's givens as a model for their workouts. I see it all the time and hear about this constantly. Someone reads a feature article in a magazine about the latest Kenyan superstar. Invariably, the writer asks the athlete for the secret of their success and this becomes the workout du jour of the reader's training group. Big mistake.

As a coach who believes in the principle of individualization, it drives me nuts when, for example, a talented young middle-distance runner tries to copy Bannister's workout and then doesn't understand why he can't run under 4:00 for the mile. Well, that workout needs to be put into the proper context of Bannister's overall training plan.

Where did he get the endurance to manage 10 × 440 with just 2:00 rest in the first place? Where did he get the speed to run 10 × 440 in 59 seconds with 2:00 rest and not have to sprint 100% all-out on each one? After all, on race day, he wasn't going to sprint for one whole mile nonstop. He needed to run each 440 in 60 seconds while finding it relaxing enough so that a 2:00 rest after each quarter-mile wasn't required.

Bannister had enough experience to know that running 10 × 440 were good givens. He also knew that he could recover within 2:00 of jogging. So he picked time (pace) as his variable knowing that he needed to develop the stamina to run four 60-second quarter-miles in a row to meet his goal. So, his first task was to get in good enough shape to be able to just finish 10 quarter-mile repeats while being able to recover from each effort with just a 2 minute rest. His fall cross-country training accomplished that endurance phase of his conditioning. His cross-country races then conditioned him well enough to begin a rather advanced second phase of conditioning. Thus, his interval workouts had to contain a mixture of pace work and speedwork if they were to prepare him to break the 4:00 minute barrier. More about the speedwork in the next two sections.

So for you it comes down to training smart by knowing which variable of the interval formula goes with what phase of training. And, for your comparison with the classic formula for endurance training that you saw earlier, here is how we design a stamina building workout for Phase II:

Unknown number of repeats × *given distance to be repeated* in *given time* at *80-85%* with *jog to 65%.*

Now, there is nothing secret or magic about selecting the givens. You simply have to decide the objective of the workout and then arbitrarily fill in the blanks with numbers that will get the job done. Just remember to leave something blank until after the workout is over. It will be over when you can't meet the limits you've set with the givens.

By now you may be questioning why Bannister's sample workout does not conform to the above model. Why didn't he just start running his 440s in 60 seconds and see how many he could do the first time? Then he could have tried to increase the number each week until he got all ten of them in under 60.

In either case, it doesn't matter as long as there is only one variable. He chose *time* knowing that he had several months to lower it to 59:9. I would have chosen the number of repeats knowing that he had several months to increase it to ten. Runners, coaches and lawyers — always looking for loopholes to explain away apparent contradictions, aren't we?

9

EXPERIMENT 3: VARIABLES AND GIVENS FOR ECONOMY AND SPEED

As we get closer to discussing the primary use of interval training by today's runners, let me digress and deal with some of the issues surrounding this type of training. In this section, I want to closely examine how intervals are used to develop the economy and speed components of conditioning. The typical workouts used for these purposes have created as many misconceptions about interval training as there were creative accounting practices going on at Enron.

To most runners, interval training is often synonymous with speedwork. If you are an adult-onset athlete, you have probably heard horror stories from runners who do speed workouts. The thought of going to the track for an interval workout probably frightens you. And if you have done one improperly, you were probably traumatized for life by the pain, torture, and agony, an experience so common that I refer to it as "The Other PTA Syndrome." Perhaps this is why the phrase "speed kills" is so popular within the running community.

Many former high school and college runners have stories that also contribute to the bad reputation of interval training. Countless poor souls were the victims of mad scientists who didn't use the one-variable-per-experiment formula when designing their athletes' interval workouts. And, compounding the insult, coaches often failed to individualize workouts according to each runner's ability, current fitness, and personal goals. Standard operating procedure for most coaches or training groups is to have everyone trying to run the same workout. That the resulting training sessions turn into multiple, mini-races amongst members of the group is inevitable. Unfortunately, racing each 400-meter repeat during a Thursday workout of 12 × 400 instead of staying within the ideal effort range of 90–95%, usually just leaves everyone but the best runners totally trashed. To recover by a Saturday race, especially if this is the second or third hard workout of the week, is simply not possible.

These misconceptions and misuse have left the image of interval training as being something that only elite runners can tolerate. It's true that runners must work hard, push themselves, learn to be tough, and find out how to ignore the body's fatigue when the mind is shouting, "Slow down, dammit!" Ironically, nothing teaches these lessons better than proper interval workouts, plus racing. Yes, *racing* is the best way to get into perfect shape. Those are the times to push oneself to a drop-dead-from-exhaustion-at-the-finish-line 100% effort. That's why you often hear wise coaches and veteran runners say that racing is the best way to get in shape to race. In fact, that's the reason for seasons.

Several to a dozen races during the fall cross-country or spring track season are the perfect compliment to a runner's interval workouts, which almost always should not exceed 90–95% in training. By limiting the effort to that level, runners will be fresh and frisky for their races, eager to take off and keep up with the leaders, or at least maintain their goal pace. Runners who try to win the workout by racing the stopwatch or their training partners may indeed be Tuesday/Thursday heroes. However, when the real competition starts, their dead legs force them to exert mighty, all-out 100% efforts too early in the race. Sprinters may be able to run all-out for up to 200 meters, but distance runners have to pace themselves and gradually let the effort creep up to 100% by the very last 200 to 400 meters of their distance races. Being able to kick it in over that distance requires a good sense of pace so a runner doesn't hit 100% exhaustion so early that the body has no choice but to slow down to a jog or a walk.

Not wanting to sound completely negative, let me point out that one of the primary benefits of properly run interval workouts is a perfectly developed *sense of pace.* By breaking up the racing distance into short segments, a runner can repeatedly practice running at specific, planned paces. Since these workouts tend to be run on the track, constant feedback in the form of frequent split times is available. Splits can be read as often as every 100 meters because all tracks have the exchange zones marked for the 4 × 100-meter relay. This quickly allows the runner to get back on the planned pace either by slowing down a bit or speeding up a tad. The *pacing skills* thus developed by interval training can be uncanny. Frequently, veteran runners can run a lap, turn to their coach before hearing their split time and announce to a tenth of a second how fast they just ran for the repeat. A secondary benefit of interval workouts is the training you get as a mathematician. You'll soon be a whiz at dividing by four.

By including the distance covered during the recovery jog, the total of the repeats usually adds up to at least three miles for middle-distance runners, but not more than six miles for long-distance runners like marathoners.

This brings me to the point I urgently need to make about which variables are the most important in interval workouts designed for economy and speed development. Take a moment to review what has been said previously about endurance and stamina workouts. Which part of the experimental formula will be the variable for an economy workout? And then, what variable would you set for a speed workout?

Did you just jump up and shout, "Coach, for economy it's got to be the effort!" If so, stick a gold star on your forehead because you just correctly answered the hardest question in the world of running. If the goal of interval workout is to develop economy, then the most important *given* is *pace* while the *variable* is *effort.* Once you have decided how fast you should run, you then arbitrarily pick the distance of your repeats. Next, your math skills will tell you how many of these repeats it will take to total the amount of *distance* you need to run for the workout. (Hint: see two paragraphs above.) With your givens now in place, a sample of the classic formula looks like this:

12 × 400 meters in *87 seconds* at *?% effort*
with a *200-meter jog recovery.*

Therefore, for a workout designed to make sure a runner is "getting better," the question is this: Can the workout be done within the range of 90–95% effort? Check the pace and effort charts. Notice that the workout is designed to improve the competitive fitness level of a runner who is in shape to race, depending what distance he has been training for, say, a mile in 5:29, a 5k in 18:47, or even a 10k in 39:00. The key is to measure how hard it is for the runner to do each repeat 400-meters. *This is best done with a heart rate monitor.* If not, then the runner better have an exquisite perception of the exertion and be able to distinguish between running hard at no more than 95% and running all-out at 100% drop-dead-from-exhaustion effort. After the workout is finished, the effort of each repeat is examined. Just like a race, they should have started at around 90% and, over the course of the workout, gone up to 95% by the last few repeats. If the effort was lower than expected, the runner must be in better shape than expected. If the effort was harder than 95% most of the time, then the runner was racing in practice and fooling himself about how fast he should finish the next race.

While the following discussion is rather moot for most long-distance runners, I do need to mention what to do when middle-distance runners like milers and half-milers have a need for speed. Without further ado, here is the formula for the experiment designed to improve a runner's speed.

Number *of repeats* × **distance** in **time** at
percent of **effort** with **??** *recovery* **interval**

A sample for a runner like the one above, would look like this:

10 × *200 meters* in *36 seconds* at *100%* effort with a **??** *jog*

How long the runner takes to recover depends on the length of time it takes to catch his breath, screw up his courage, and be ready to take off again. And, if it takes longer to begin the next repeat, that's okay because this is not an endurance-, stamina-, or economy-building workout. The objective is to *run fast without getting hurt*. Therefore, it is absolutely not important to start again after a fixed distance or fixed time or fixed activity interval, whether ready or not.

If you were following the typically incorrect formula for the above sample workout, the distance of the interval would probably be fixed at a distance chosen by the coach. If you tried to follow that inflexible formula for failure, your pace would have to suffer because there is no alternative to fatigue that reaches 100% during the repeat, except to slow down.

By beginning your next repeat before you've fully recovered to the ideal of at least 60%, you would be getting more and more tired earlier and earlier on each repeat. Once at full exhaustion, your times for the repeat 200s would have to vary and that, folks, is the *wrong* variable.

If your goal is to run fast, why teach yourself how to slow down? Instead just take more and more time between repeats as the workout progresses. It's okay — it's the variable. Having one variable per interval workout is the real secret to success.

True middle-distance runners should refer back to chapter 6.

10

SUMMING UP INTERVAL WORKOUTS

Interval training is, hands down, the best way to develop fast feet. Why? Because the workouts can be done in a nice, scientifically controlled way. These all-important controls are the best way to avoid that dreaded disease, The Fast-feet, Slow-mind Syndrome.

Let me start by explaining why you would choose one interval workout over another. By reviewing the objectives of the phases of training, we'll put these trackside experiments into the proper context so you will know how to arrange the variable and the givens.

There is no question that in order to compete at their best, runners must put themselves through the following four phases of training:

> **Phase I: Getting in Shape.** This is the two- to three-month period of jogging and easy aerobic efforts that develop *endurance*, the ability to finish the distance commensurate with the length of the goal races, no matter

how much one must slow down, but without walking.

Phase II: Getting Ready to Race. This is the four- to six-week period of steady and threshold running that develops *stamina,* the ability to maintain race pace for races like 10ks and longer.

Phase III: Getting Better. This is the phase of training that lasts two to four months of the racing season and develops *economy,* the ability of the working muscles to use as little energy and oxygen as possible at racing paces.

Phase IV: Getting Ready to Peak. This is a two- to four-week phase that develops *speed,* the ability to run faster than race pace so a runner can stay relaxed as racing paces get faster and faster on the way to personal records and championship events.

Even though very few runners use interval training these days to develop endurance, check the charts below to see how you can manipulate the givens and the variables in order to develop all four components of conditioning. But first review this . . .

THE UNIVERSAL INTERVAL WORKOUT FORMULA

Number *of* *repeats*	×	*Distance of* **repeats**	in	**time**	at	*Percent of* **effort**	with	*Time/activity of* **interval**

Now notice how that formula changes according to the objectives of the workout.

ENDURANCE WORKOUT FORMULA

Given								
number						*Given*		
of repeats		*Given*		*Variable*		*% of*		*Given*
to 70%	×	**distance**	in	**time**	at	**effort**	with	**interval**

For example: 20 × 400m in **??** time at 75–80% effort with 200m jog.

STAMINA WORKOUT FORMULA

Variable						*Given*		
number		*Given*		*Given*		*% of*		*Given*
of repeats	×	**distance**	in	**time**	at	**effort**	with	**interval**

For example: **??** × 1,600 in 6:00 at 80–85% effort with 400m jog.

ECONOMY WORKOUT FORMULA

Given								
time						*Variable*		
number		*Given*		*Given*		*% of*		*Given*
of repeats	×	**distance**	in	**time**	at	**effort**	with	**interval**

For example: 12 x 400m in 75 sec. at **??** effort with 200m jog.

SPEED WORKOUT FORMULA

Given						*Given*		
number		*Given*		*Given*		*% of*		*Variable*
of repeats	×	**distance**	*in*	**time**	*at*	**effort**		**interval**

For example: 8 × 200m in 32 sec. at 100% effort with **??** minutes of rest.

Since I consider it my mission as coach to turn the theoretical into the practical for application on the track and trails, let me convert the above abstract examples into real life examples. The following workouts were run by 41-year-old Kellie Eyre, my top female masters runner, in preparation for the mile at the National Masters Indoors Championships in 2002. The previous summer she had run 4:49 for 1,500m to place sixth at the World Masters Championships in Brisbane, Australia. Her goal for the 2002 indoor meet was to run from three to seven seconds faster than her time at the 2001 meet, where she ran 5:07.

Kellie used the more modern Lydiard system of off-track easy-distance running for developing her endurance. So the following examples start with her stamina workouts.

During Phase II, the givens and variables looked like this:

Number of Repeats	Distance of Repeats	Time Allotted	% of Effort	Rest Interval
??	1,600m	6:15	80–85%	400m to allow recovery to 70%

In formula format, she ran: **??** × 1,600 in 6:15 at 80–85% with 400m jog When she could run three repeats, we moved on to Phase III.

During Phase III, the givens and variables looked like this:

Number of Repeats	Distance of Repeats	Time Allotted	% of Effort	Rest Interval
12	400m	1:20	**??**	200m to allow recovery to 65%

In formula format, she ran 12 × 400m in 1:20 at **??** effort with a 200m jog. When she could run all the 400s while staying within the 90–95% effort zone, we moved on to Phase IV.

During Phase IV, the givens and variables looked like this:

Number of Repeats	Distance of Repeats	Time Allotted	% of Effort	Rest Interval
10	200m	:33.5	100%	**??** to allow recovery to 60%

In the fomula format, she ran 10 × 200 in 33:5 seconds at 100% effort with **??** walking as she needed between repeats in order to be fully recovered. Since she got increasingly tired as the workout progressed, she took longer and longer time between repeats to get down to at least 60%, lower if she needed. That was perfectly okay because maintaining other aspects of her conditioning were not the objective of this workout. This workout's goal was to develop her leg speed and live to tell about it by running very fast for a few short repeats without injuring something.

So there you have my interpretation of the science behind Interval Training. That's my story and I'm sticking with it. I told my wife that I was in the hammock on the back porch all night figuring this out and she believed me. I hope you do, too. It will shorten your learning curve from the lifetime that it has taken me to understand this beautiful system for training runners to go fast.

MARATHON TRAINING

11

MARATHON TRAINING

If the 1960s were The Age of Aquarius, the '90s were the Age of Marathoners. Thanks to all the self-appointed gurus, charity-driven training programs and the new breed of private, certified coaches in business today, marathoning has become to fitness what jogging did for health back in the 1970s.

Unfortunately, finishing a marathon with a big smile in one's goal time is not an easy task. For many runners, it is a miserable experience. Even well-executed race strategies, run in perfect weather in well-organized races can require weeks of recovery.

I mention this to prepare you for disappointment that follows. I cannot offer detailed training programs for marathoners because I cannot do so honestly. No book can do so. Each runner is too different and there are too many goal times involving too many ranges of effort. So call me if you want some coaching. Read on if you want suggestions for two key workouts for every runner wishing to get the damn thing over with as quickly as possible.

THE SCIENCE OF 80/90 WORKOUT FOR MARATHONERS

For marathoners planning to imporve their PRs for the daunting 26.2 mile race, I suggest two special workouts:

1. Running from 6–13 miles (or in cases of truly veteran, advanced marathoners, up to 18 miles) at Planned Marathon Pace (PMP).
2. Interval workouts of 6–12 × 800 at Yasso pace.

These specialized workouts are the basis of my 80/90 workout plan. However, successful execution of these workouts requires a little background information.

Intense physical tests such as the marathon have always benefited from the use of tools and "helpers." The most significant of these helpers came about the late 1960s, when Dr. Robert Cade, a kidney specialist at the University of Florida Medical School in Gainesville, had one of the greatest ideas in the history of sports medicine and exercise science.

While watching the Gator football players wilt in the southern heat and humidity, he wondered if he could help them avoid heat exhaustion and the deterioration of performance associated with dehydration by replacing their lost sweat. His solution — pun intended — developed into Gatorade, a perfect example of the scientific mind at its inquisitive best. Over the years, Doc Cade's conclusions have been validated by the countless other experiments that good science requires. These, in turn, have led to constant refinement of fluid and energy replacement drinks to the point where we now have nutrient-laden Accelerade, which allows us to digest a virtual meal on the run.

While Dr. Cade's development provided us with hydration fluids that also expand our energy supply, a new generation of tools is providing more scientific ways to control our training.

That scientific control can come from three sources: 1) a new, magic gizmo with the potential of having the same revolutionary effect that Gatorade did; 2) an old one used by many, but often not fully and accurately utilized; and 3) a familiar tool newly revised just for marathoners.

The new gizmo is a speed and distance monitor. Working just like your car's speedometer, it tells you with uncanny accuracy how fast you are running and how far you have gone. It's not a pedometer that just counts your predetermined measured steps. The best one, the sdm/triax® made by NIKE, uses accelerometers housed in a pod attached to your shoe to measure the force and frequency of each stride. So, while constantly sending signals to a wrist receiver about your pace, they also measure each 1/100th of every mile that you run. NIKE's [techlab™ has developed a new model that adds heart rate monitoring and is now on the market.

The old source of control is the heart rate monitor, which has been around since the early 1980s. Please review everything I have written in the earlier sections of this book about training with a heart rate monitor. Those comments are even more important for marathoners: you cannot do these workouts without a monitor. You'll soon see why.

The third handy tool is familiar to both of you who bought my earlier book, *The Runner's Coach,* and offers even more scientific control. It is the pace chart originally developed by Coach Extraordinaire Jack Daniels. I have used it for over fifteen years as the cornerstone of my effort-based training philosophy. Coach Daniels graciously allowed my "effort" modifications so I could correlate his training paces with how hard or easy runners are working. The percentages of maximum effort can then be converted by the Target Heart Rate calculator in Table C into beats per minute to be shown on a heart rate monitor. Being a rather scientific-minded coach who has used heart rate monitors for many years to help runners train more intelligently, I think I've found a new way to correlate the charts to the efforts that marathoners need. Read on.

Bart Yasso may not have the credentials of a physician or a physiologist. However, he is just as much a genius as Doc Cade. Bart has the same empirical powers that allow someone to observe a relationship and then wonder if there is some general truth about it. His discovery is now known to marathoners everywhere as Yasso 800s, a speed workout of 10 × 800 meters with a couple of minutes' rest interval. These workouts are one of the two special marathon workouts I mentioned earlier.

Bart noticed that the resulting average time of the 800s, in minutes and seconds, has the power to predict a marathoner's finish time in hours and minutes. Finding this correlation with his own workouts, he started asking other marathoners about their speedwork. Veteran runners, with a full range of marathon times, but familiar enough with interval training to have done similar workouts, checked their logs. And, sure enough, they found the same correlation. With that, Yasso 800s were born and popularized. However, it's now time for other scientists to validate Yasso's conclusion. I think that I've found a way to validate Yasso's 800 workout by putting a few controls on his experiment.

So, here's an offer: How would you like to be pretty sure, if not positive, that you are training properly in order to meet your marathon time goal? Or, putting it differently, how would you like to know if your goal is realistic or idealistic? If so, here's an invitation to sacrifice your body in the name of science. No, not really, I'm just kidding.

Start by checking out the chart of 80/90 Workouts for Marathoners in Tables H1 and H2. But hold it! Don't try using it without first reading the following explanation. The chart, like your running, a work-in-progress and could very well bamboozle you just like your digital camera did when you tried to take pictures without reading the instructions. So please study it carefully. You'll find that the 80/90 chart is a special variation of that old chestnut "Coach Benson's Pace and Effort Chart." My long-time coaching client, Paul Daniele, compiled it. Paul is an Engineer of the First Order and a Frustrated Physiologist of High Amateur Rank. He has the same astute empirical powers as the aforementioned geniuses, Cade & Yasso. While I was talking with Paul one day about the amazing accuracy of Yasso 800s, he happened to notice that the times fell into the 90% effort column of my original chart. Suddenly it dawned on me that here was the answer to a question that had been nagging me about Yasso's workout: how hard should the 800s be? All-out at 100% maximum effort? As easy as a walk in the park at 75% effort? Since they were regarded as "speedwork," they obviously had to be faster than goal pace, but how much faster? Well, we suspect that the answer is found in the 90% column on the line of your current 10k level of fitness.

Still one more question begged an answer: how much recovery should there be in the interval between the repeat 800s? To standardize the workout, I recommend jogging between 200–400 meters at a pace easy enough to allow your heart rate to return to 70%, and not any lower!

Paul was also responsible for another brilliant observation. While studying my Pace & Effort chart for Distance Runners (Table B), he noticed an interesting relationship between a runner's current 10k level of fitness and their marathon race pace. Dropping down one line below the current 10k time and then reading to the right, Paul found their effort at marathon pace was 80%.

Before you try the Yasso workout, keep in mind that every interval workout is nothing more than an experiment to test fitness. And, remember that solid science requires that there be only one variable per workout. With these Yasso half-miles, the distance of the repeats is given, the pace is given, the effort is given, and the interval is given, thereby leaving only the number as the variable.

Plan to run the workout every other week of your marathon training period. Start with four and add one each time to reach ten repeats two weeks before your marathon. See the Marathon

Training Plan in Table I and notice how this is incorporated with the other workouts. To determine your pace for these repeat half miles, look at the 90% column for your current level of 10k fitness in Table H1. The goal is to stay close to a 90% effort while running at the pace in the 90% column. To realize the predictive value, you should be able to run 10–12 × 800 yards by the end of your preparation period.

You have probably noticed from the chart that we have had to resort to some Coachly Fudging in order to recognize that not all marathoners are built the same. Over a distance this long, runners with lots of slow-twitch muscles have a marked advantage over runners whose higher percent of fast-twitch fibers make them better suited to middle distances like the 5k and the mile. If you're not sure if you are more of a marathoner than middle-distance runner, take this test: do you enjoy more racing success over 5k or 15k? If you choose 5k, you probably have more fast twitch fibers. If you seem to do better over 15k, 10 miles, or even the half marathon, it's probably due to having more slow twitch muscles.

As a result of these individual differences, we have distinguished between what we feel would be realistic and ideal race times and training paces. You pure marathoners should use the ideal columns while you sprinter types will find the realistic columns more to your liking.

Because of the valid correlations between fitness, pace, and effort, there are several ways to use the pace chart. You already know that if you can run "x" time for 10k, then across the chart from that time, under the 90% column, are the times you should run for your mile speedwork. Maybe you don't have any idea what kind of 10k shape you're in. But if you can run a batch of eight to ten 880s in "y" time at 90 percent effort, then the average time of those 880s will tell you what kind of time to expect in the marathon and, conversely, what kind of shape you must be in for a 10k. At any rate, one thing should be made perfectly clear: you must use a heart rate monitor to measure this effort to be sure that you are not under- or over-training. Hey, I don't call it effort-based training for nothing.

For your Planned Marathon Pace (PMP) runs, the 80% column offers the pace you should follow on these runs they will increase in length from five or six to as many as 13 miles over the period of your Training Plan. PMP runs are prescribed as an excellent way to develop the comfort and biomechanical familiarity with the pace you must run on race day. The Training Plan shows how these should be included in your weekly mileage.

Pure marathoners would use the ideal 80% paces listed, while shorter distance specialists, would use the realistic 80% pace, which in reality is more like 77–78% effort. If wearing a heart monitor, do not exceed a heart rate greater than 80% of your training range. Much of your PMP runs should be in the 78–79% range, only reaching 80% near the end as additional muscle fibers are recruited to respond to the onset of fatigue. If you begin to exceed 80%, slow down. Of course, your heart rate at the start of your PMP run should be well below your 78% target. It may take several miles of goal pace running to reach that upper limit, just like in a race when you're fresh at the beginning. The only exceptions to this are elite runners who can, on occasion, exceed an 80% effort.

There is another thing that should have caught your attention. I have deliberately switched from metric measurements by now referring to half miles and their equivalents, 880 yards. See Chapter 8 for a discussion of why this is important. We run metric distances on the roads except, naturally, for that most English of distances, the marathon. So, since that's the case, why not practice at exactly the same English splits? Being thirty feet short each mile may not seem like much but it could result in a sense of pace that is off enough to keep you from qualifying for Boston someday.

Of course, the answer to this specificity challenge is the NIKE line of pace/distance/HR monitors. Since the monitors measure your mileage in miles, there is another advantage that should be clear by now: you can run all your 80/90 workouts on the roads anywhere, not just your local certified race courses. Better yet, no more dizzying laps around a track or adding fifteen feet to each 800m run to convert it to the longer 880 yards. The freedom of the roads also offers the challenges of hills, a feature found on many a marathon course. Talk about learning how to pace yourself and parcel out the proper effort. Is this a brave new world or what?

MORE COACHLY WISDOM

12

HEART RATE MONITOR TIPS

Here are some general day-to-day helpful hints on using your heart monitor in training.

- When warming up or down, keep your heart rate in the 60–65% effort zone for at least five minutes.

- To avoid the Dreaded First Wind, do not exceed 70% effort until you start sweating and are fully warmed up, loose, and ready to go to town.

- To enjoy the Friendly Second Wind, gradually take your heart rate up from your warm-up zone to 75–80% and hold it there just below your anaerobic threshold throughout your run. This effort zone is known as a "steady-state" run. It's everybody's favorite training pace and effort because it's biomechanically comfortable and still aerobic enough to allow conversation, at least in short distances.

- If you run primarily to control your weight, keep your heart rate in the 60–70% zone the entire time in order to maximize your muscle's use of fat as its main fuel. Walk or jog at least six or even seven days per week for at least 45 to 60 minutes per day.

- If you run primarily to keep your heart healthy, do two or three heart rate fartlek workouts per week. Just run your heart rate like a roller coaster up and down between 70 and 85% of effort. This period of picking up and slowing down your speed should last for 15 to 20 minutes per workout, not including warm-up and warm-down time.

- If you run several times per week, you should follow a hard/easy pattern of training. Run hard by going longer or faster on one day. Recover by running shorter or slower on the next day. Fast running is in the 80–95% effort zone. Slow runs are in the 60 to 75% zone. If you prefer to run comfortable, steady-state runs every day at a constant 75 to 80% effort, alternate between long and short runs.

- If you are a "social" runner, be sure that your partner(s) matches your fitness and ability level. Your target HRs may be different, but they have to be in the same % effort zone.

- If you run primarily to have a strong, healthy heart and to also finish an occasional 5 or 10k without getting so exhausted that you have to slow down to a crawl, you should push the anaerobic threshold of 85% for five minutes two or three times per workout a couple of times per week.

- If you want to train to finish a marathon with a smile on your face, keep all of your mileage between 60–75% MHR, especially on your long runs.

SOME ADDITIONAL THOUGHTS AND OBSERVATIONS

Runs of 30-45 minutes and longer in warm weather and humidity may cause your THR to increase ten to fifteen bpms as you become dehydrated and your heart is recruited to run your radiator (cooling through sweating) system. On easy days this may happen without any apparent increase in your level of perceived exertion until your decreased blood volume causes a significant increase in heart rate and then a decrease in your cardiac output. At this point you'll notice how hard it suddenly has become to maintain your pace. Don't fight it — just slow down and keep your heart rate below 75%. I call this response "cardiac creep." Fast, hard efforts on warm, humid days will simply result in slower paces.

The opposite of cardiac creep is "cardiac crimp." It happens on cold days when it isn't necessary to turn on your radiator and top sweat in order to cool off. Thus, your HR stays wonderfully low and you get to run "effortlessly" faster on your hard days. That's why Khalid Kannouchi keeps setting world records on those freezing days in Chicago. On your easy days, don't let cardiac crimp seduce you into running faster than the pace/effort charts allow.

Paradoxically, you won't come near your actual MHR by

sprinting all-out or running hard up a hill, unless you do so after 15 to 20 minutes of steady running. Initial bursts of speed load your muscles with so much lactic acid that they fail before your HR reaches maximum. Hence the need for a graded treadmill stress test, or a similar field test, to determine your maximum heart rate.

Also paradoxically, your training heart rate won't always increase to match your perceived level of exertion. Sometimes your legs won't have recovered fully from the previous workout and you simply won't have the energy to run fast enough to elevate your heart rate to usual levels.

If you run competitively in 5k races, your heart rate should be close to 90% by the end of the first mile and then go up slightly over the next two miles, hitting 95% or more at the finish.

If you run competitively in 10k races, your heart rate should be near 85% by the end of the first mile. Over the next three miles it will increase to 90–95% if you don't give in and slow down.

In a 15k, your heart rate should be near 80% in at the first mile and average 85% for the remainder of the race.

In a half marathon, you should hold you heart rate in the 75–80% range for the first few miles and allow it to increase into the low 80s for the remainder.

13

BIOMECHANICS WITHOUT TEARS

It's fair to compare a runner's cardiorespiratory system to a car's engine. So, let's take the analogy one step further and compare the runner's muscloskeletal system to a car's transmission and wheels. In this chapter, instead of viewing runners from the physiological, biochemical, or psychological perspective, we'll look at their biomechanics—their arms and legs.

If the physiological systems need to be trained to be *economical* in their use of energy and oxygen, then I think it's fair to assert that the biomechanical systems can be fine-tuned to assure *efficient* movement. Bear with me, a wise veteran coach who is also an old low-rent exercise scientist. We're dealing with words with multiple meanings and I don't want purists to be splitting my semantical hairs here.

Unfortunately, while exercise scientists of all specialties have studied the fine art of running fast and published their contributions, there is no standard, commonly agreed upon vocabulary to connect their ivory tower laboratory jargon with the our basement locker room language. It seems to me that physiologists and "biomechanicists" share words that sometimes mean different things to each other. They may also mean something different to us coaches. So, gentle runner, be forewarned that things may get a tad confusing. Not with me, but with other things that you may have read or heard. For example, I believe that one's efficiency of movement can impact how economically one runs. However, becoming more economical through training doesn't make a runner with poor form more efficient. In short, it can be a case of form over substance. To me, a runner with bad form is inefficient because some energy is being wasted on movements that negatively impact the forward progress. But an efficient runner with good form who is simply in poor shape can be uneconomical because far more muscle fibers have to be recruited to do the job. Just as a runner with poor form also has to recruit more fibers to get the job done uneconomically. See what I mean?

So let's simplify all this by saying that *economy of motion* concerns how much energy is required by the working muscles to run a given pace, while *efficiency of motion* concerns how little energy is wasted at that pace by form faults.

Let's get down to business and identify a few of these common problems with form. These are biomechanical mistakes that are easily corrected by a few simple drills. The result is a more efficient runner who uses less oxygen and energy to run at the same pace, thus becoming more economical. Doesn't this make sense now? Good. If not, press on anyway and the hell with the language. Just let me try to share some coachly wisdom by showing you how to identify bad form.

You have to start with some film of yourself. There are two ways to do this: 1) Pay big bucks to get filmed and analyzed by a high-rent professional coach who knows biomechanics. Or 2) Get a friend or relative with a video camera to film you, then do the analysis yourself by following these simple instructions. Trust me, it's not that hard because these common form faults are glaringly easy to identify.

Start by going to a local track with someone who can operate the zoom on the video camera without cutting off your feet. Have them film you according to the following protocols so there will be three views: front, rear, and side. (See how easy this is?)

The first two views can be recorded by doing the following:

1. Station the cameraman in a middle lane of the track between two white lane lines about halfway down the straight-away 50 meters from you. Have him zoom in on you for a close-up view of you facing the camera.
2. Run at about 5k pace down the same lane that the cameraman is in.
3. As you run, have the cameraman back off the zoom keeping as much of you in full frame as possible.
4. When you get too close to be in full view, have the cameraman focus on the upper half of your body so your arm and shoulder action can be analyzed. Stop directly in front of the camera and turn around while the cameraman keeps the close-up focus on your back, shoulders, and head.
5. Upon command, run back down to the starting point allowing the camera to first film the rear view of your upper body and then your entire height as you run fully into view.

Important warning: have the cameraman rewind the film and play it back while checking his results in the viewfinder. This is very critical in order to avoid the same incredible embarrassment that I have suffered on more than one occasion when I had reversed the filming process by not noticing that the camera was already on when I pressed the record button. This, of course, meant that I had turned the camera off when I wanted it on and then turned it on when I wanted it off, resulting in no record of the test runs. I have had, however, lots of nice shots of the sky and ground that I did not know the camera recorded because I wasn't paying attention. This double check will also allow you to repeat the test process if you are not happy with the quality of the picture. Hey, practice makes perfect, so don't complain. Remember, this could be something that your grandchildren may come across when they inherit your estate. You'll be happy that you went to the extra trouble to look good for them.

If everything is okay, continue as follows to film the side view:

1. Move the cameraman onto the infield of the track about 10 to 15 yards from the inside edge of the first lane.
2. Position him about 25 yards closer to you so the camera is halfway between you and the finish point of your run.
3. Stay in the middle lane of the track so the curb on the inner edge of the track won't block the view of your foot strike.
4. Make three passes back and forth over this 50 yard distance at the following paces:
   - jogging
   - running at 5k race pace
   - "kicking" or running at almost a full-speed sprint

   (These three round trips will result in views of both your left and right sides.)
5. Be sure that the cameraman has you zoomed in at the start of your run. As you draw closer, he should back off the zoom in order to keep you in full view, not cutting off your feet. If he lops off your head, OK. But your feet need to be in the picture so we can analyze your foot strike.

Again, review the tape to see how it came out. Repeat the

process if the quality is not real clear, especially when you are close to being perpendicular to the camera. Those three to four strides as you go directly in front of the camera are crucial.

I hope you can tell from all this detailed description that you are going to experience some high-speed excitement here. I also hope that you can understand the need for a good warm-up before you star in this home movie. You want to be sure that you don't wind up on "America's Funniest Home Videos" by doing a forward half flip onto your back when you pull your hamstring during the sprint down the track. Jog at least a mile, do your stretches, and run a few strides before you start the filming.

Amazingly, all these instructions are the easy part of this scientific exercise. Now comes the hard part: seeing yourself on film. You will probably be surprised to find out that you do not look as graceful as Suzy Hamilton or as powerful as Michael Johnson. I hope this dash of reality won't be too hard to absorb as you put the film in the VCR and look for the form faults illustrated below:

THE FAULT: EXCESSIVE UPPER BODY ROTATION

If you are guilty, you are wasting energy as your top half twists around above your hips much like a washing machine agitator swishes back and forth. This causes your upper body to turn in partial circles (rotary motion) instead of following the lower half along the straight line (linear motion) that you are trying to run. Runners with this fault are often seen letting their right wrist fly away from their side, usually in a flawed attempt to relax the arms and shoulders. The elbow then swings around behind the back, thus pulling the right shoulder back along with it. This much rotary force usually causes the opposite hand and arm to cross over the runner's front midline, pulling that shoulder forward and adding to the rotary twist.

Consequently, in an effort to keep the runner on a straight course instead of veering off in the direction the upper body is pointing, the forward leg must compensate by slightly crossing over the midline (the imaginary line down the center of your trunk from your nose to your belly button). This extra motion of the adductor muscles wastes more valuable energy. Moreover, strains to the iliotibial tendon, which runs from the top of the waist bone down over the hip joint and then along the outside of the leg to where it attaches below the knee, are often caused by this unnecessary hyperextension of the hip and leg.

Check your video to see if your film shows any of these form faults. (If you have slow-motion capacity on your VCR, slight faults will be greatly magnified so don't despair too much if you look really spastic.)

THE CORRECTION

Before trying to eliminate this problem by using the simple drill described below, please consider the objective: you want to stop swinging your shoulders back and forth. This is done by keeping your arms close to the side of your trunk by lightly brushing the inside of your wrists against your shirt as your arms swing back and forth in a relaxed, but slightly diagonal direction right below your ribs. Let your hands swing forward to, but not across, the midline of your body. On the backswing of your arm, let your hand go all the way back even with your hip. As you keep your wrist in contact with your shirt, you'll notice that your elbow swings back and away from your side, but not your forearm. You will probably feel like you are elbowing someone next to you right in the stomach or chest, sort of like you're trying to keep them from passing you. Later when you're out on a test run trying out your new form, concentrate on this change by repeating part of this old

Ipana toothpaste jingle, "brusha, brusha, brusha." Keep brushing your inner wrist against your shirt.

To bring about these changes, begin changing your form by standing in front of a mirror. Let your arms hang down along your side with your shoulders as relaxed as you can possibly make them. Then pretend that you are in a western movie and you are going to draw your six shooters and point them at the outlaws. Do this by bending your arms at the elbows, raising your forearms until they're level with the ground, and then point your index finger straight at the bad guy. Next, lift your thumbs so they are pointing straight up, as when we used our hands to imitate a gun when we were little shavers playing cowboys.

Now stop playing cowboys by bending your index finger back into your fist while still keeping your thumbs pointing straight up in a 12 o'clock position. Next, think like a clock and rotate your right wrist slightly until your thumb is pointing at 10 o'clock. Do the opposite with the left wrist so you've rotated your forearm enough to get your thumb pointed to 2 o'clock.

The rotation of your wrists is absolutely crucial to this drill because it allows your forearm to swing naturally back and forth while keeping the shoulder muscles completely relaxed.

Now, you should find that it is your arms, *not your shoulders,* that are alternately swinging back and forth, hand to hip, elbow to hip, in rhythm with your stride. To the mantra, "brusha, brusha, brusha" add, "ten to two." It should come out something like, "At ten to two remember to brusha, brusha, brusha."

THE FAULT: OVERSTRIDING

After all that talk about upper body rotation, you might be surprised that the most common biomechanical mistake made by joggers and runners is over-striding. This mistake results in a simple waste of energy because they are actually putting on their brakes with each footstrike.

Gross overstriding occurs when the foot strikes the ground heel first, with the leg straight and the knee locked, way in front of the runner's center of gravity. At the moment of contact, a runner's lead leg has to absorb anywhere from one and one-half to four times body weight (depending on the pace) from the impact of returning to earth after that exhilarating trip through the air when both feet are off the ground. Obviously, the greater the speed and the longer the time in the air, the greater the impact. No matter how slow the runner is going, when the forces are absorbed up and through a straight lead leg, the effect is one of putting on the brakes. Because of the "equal and opposite reaction" law of physics, when a 150-pound runner, for example, traveling at five minutes per mile, obeys gravity and comes back down to earth, the heel is jammed into the ground causing from 450 to 600 pounds of force to reverse the angle of impact. These impact forces go straight back up the leg at an angle opposite of the direction the runner is trying to travel. This has a braking effect on the forward progress, keeping the pace slower than expected for a given energy expenditure.

Not only is this a brain bouncer, but it puts even more stresses all the way up the leg through the ankle, knee, and hip joints as both the hard and soft tissues try to absorb those impact forces. As you might expect, injury risks from this type of poor form are greatly increased. Ironically, so are sales of shoes specifically designed to absorb all this unnecessary impact.

THE CORRECTION

Instead of absorbing all this punishment to the body and wallet, overstriders need to make a simple adjustment in their biomechanics to eliminate the problem.

Here's how to become flat heel strikers. Stop landing on the very back edge of your heels. Land with your leg bent and foot almost flat. By landing closer to flat-footed posture, with just an inch or two of daylight under your toe instead of the five or six inches you can see, you will avoid overstriding. You accomplish this by consciously relaxing your shin muscles allowing your toes to drop down toward the track while your foot is still in the air. This action has an opposite reaction of lifting up the heel of that foot, thereby creating more space for your leg to swing back under your bending knee. In effect, you have shortened your leg length by raising your heel to keep it from striking the ground too soon and too far out in front of you.

I have one simple drill that I use to teach my runners how make the switch from being an overstriding heel hitter to a smooth, efficient running machine. To find out if the lesson might apply to you, first check the heels of your running shoes. If they are severely worn down right along the middle of the back edge while the rest of the heel shows little evidence of wear, you have your first hint that you may be an overstrider. Normal footstrike at slow paces usually occurs more on the outside corner of the heel, so wear in that area may not indicate a tendency to overstride. If you have any doubts, try the next test.

As you analyze your videotape, look to see if you are banging the back corner of your heels on impact with the track. Watch your foot strike and see how much daylight is under the toe of the shoe at your moment of heel contact. If there appear to be several inches, then shift your focus up to your knee if see if it looks like it is locked and your leg is straight at moment of impact. Usually this affect will get more obvious and dramatic with the increase in speed. If you suspect that this may be a problem for you, try this cure: take up bike riding. No, just kidding. But those round wheels do cure the problem.

Here's the drill that I have my runners do to correct over-striding: jog in place.

Yes, that's the start. It shows you how it feels to get off your heels because no one can run in place landing heel first without feeling and looking spastic. Try it and you'll see how it feels to run like a sprinter. But rest assured that I'm not trying to turn you into a Michael Johnson. In fact, don't even try to become a mid-foot striker by landing on your toes or even on the ball of your foot. Your foot bones and tendons are not strong enough to handle the sudden switch of impact point. Instead, just try to get the feel of landing flat-heeled by pretending that you're trying to stomp on an attack bug that's heading for your other leg. You'll get this flat-footed feeling by continuing the drill from that jogging-in-place position to starting to run with this exaggerated tippy-toe foot strike. As you continue along at a comfortable running pace somewhat faster than just jogging, you will notice that you'll come down off your toes to begin landing on the balls of your feet for a couple of steps. Next, you'll notice that flat-footed feeling and finally, you'll be back on the edge of your heels.

Concentrate on this sequence as you do several of these drills for the 20 or 30 yards that it usually takes to go through this foot strike sequence. You will easily develop the kinesthetic feel of what part of your foot first strikes the ground. It will take some time doing this drill after each of your workouts to develop the coordination and strength to change your stride mechanics permanently and well enough to keep you from winding up back on your heels. But it is not a difficult adjustment to make once you feel the difference of impact in these various positions. Just keep looking for the knee to be bent when you feel the landing impact.

Eventually your running will be as smooth as silk, your foot strike as soft as cotton, and you'll feel like you're sailing along enjoying a long second wind pushing you along the way to miles of smiles.

14

MENTAL TRAINING: IT'S AN EFFORT

As that great Czechoslovakian philosopher Emil Zatopek once said, "I'll show you what 'mentally tough' means." Then he ran off with the gold medals in the 5,000 meters, the 10,000 meters and, for good measure, the marathon in the 1952 Olympics. That triple is so tough that only one other runner since then has come close to matching Zatopek's accomplishment. Lasse Viren of Finland placed fifth in the marathon at the Montreal Olympics in 1976 after defending the 5,000m and 10,000m titles he won in Munich four years earlier.

How about today's runners? We rarely hear the "No guts, no glory!" proclamation from little boys anymore, as they challenge each other to jump off the garage roof to test Mom's umbrella as a parachute. And yet, despite our soft society's "no risk" attitude, everyone still agrees that toughness is a good trait for serious athletes. Gosh, yes. And, if it's good for athletes like football players to be mentally tough, certainly runners should be tough, too. And if those gladiator guys are tough enough to play despite pain, shouldn't runners, too, be able to break through the pain barriers?

No pain, no gain, right? Yes — but with the following qualification: there's a difference between pain from an injury and the pain of fatigue. The type of pain that runners should be trying to overcome is the overwhelming tightening up of muscles that are deep in oxygen debt — not the white hot, searing, exquisite tenderness of acute or chronic injury.

Football players, as we know, are famous at enduring the second type of pain. However, they not only get hurt from those terrific hits that they put on each other, but they can also run through pain when they have to sprint full speed near the end of the game when someone runs back a punt for 100 yards.

So where does being tough mentally enter the picture?

Well, football players are evidently not as mentally tough as distance runners when it comes to dealing with exhaustion. Time after time we see these huffing and puffing players come out, sit down on the bench, and then suck on oxygen bottles. So, if they're smart enough not to "tough out" their episodes of oxygen debt exhaustion, does that mean they are — wimps?

I doubt it because we know that when it comes to playing in pain football players are the original Macho Men. They're so good at it that they often jeopardize their future health. They regularly turn acute injuries into chronic conditions by continuing to "play hurt." Boy, you talk about being mentally tough! What great role models.

However, emulating that type of toughness is the wrong thing for us runners. Running in pain from an acute or chronic injury is a very stupid thing to do. Doing it just proves that we're macho idiots who enjoy handicapping ourselves against the competition. To prove our mental toughness, we should show football players how we keep competing when the oxygen debt bears jump on our backs.

We should show them how good we are at ignoring the

incredible heaviness and tightness in our legs, stomachs, arms, shoulders, necks, and heads as the lactic acid causes the muscles to forget how to relax. To prove that we're not wimps, we need to demonstrate how to gracefully "die" down the home stretch as we desperately search for oxygen like a scuba diver sucking on a dry tank.

This means ignoring the overwhelming urge to slow down drastically or even to quit running altogether when the going gets tough near the end of a race. It means sprinting past rival racers when we'd rather slow to a jog. It means gutting it out until we've crossed the finish line.

The psychologists have labeled this behavior the act of "dissociation" and have discovered that successful athletes have this capacity in spades. The best runners simply don't admit to themselves how bad they're hurting during that long kick to the finish line. They can ignore the pain of exhaustion at the end of a race, and that's one of the things that separate them from the rest of the pack. In coaching vernacular, they're mentally tough. The trick, however, for us coaches is to teach our runners when and where it's appropriate to be mentally tough, because it's not a full-time thing.

Now you should notice that every single reference that I've had to mental toughness concerns racing situations. Coaches love runners who show up to compete at races, not at practices. "Workout winners," on the other hand, are the bane of a coach's existence. These poor, confused, misguided souls have it all backward and need to be taught that there is a big difference between conditioning the body and conditioning the mind. Heroic workouts simply aren't necessary. Training in pain from acute or chronic injuries is not heroic; it's dumb. Working out at 100% effort is also not heroic — it's misguided.

Both of those approaches sooner or later will prove to be counterproductive. If runners are hurt, they should seek medical help, not come to practice or races. If runners are overtraining, they should seek a good coach or go back over their workout logs in order to learn how to train using their heads, not their guts.

It's my contention that when injured or over-trained runners come to the starting line, they have to start using their mental toughness right from the moment that the gun goes off in order to overcome their handicaps of dead or painful legs. Fresh, well-conditioned (or even slightly under-trained) runners will then have an advantage because they won't have to push the toughness buttons until the gun lap, just when the going really gets tough.

Then we get to see the real heroes. The real heroes are the winners; those runners who win the race overall, or who win their age group, or who set personal records, or who set personal course records, or who out kick personal rivals. Winners are the real heroes because they exhibit the mental toughness that it takes to discipline themselves to do everything right, both on and off the track or roads. It sometimes takes guts to admit that training or racing with the handicap of injury or illness is not right. Skipping the workout or the race can then take more mental toughness than starting to run while knowing deep down that you can't do it and will use the handicap as an excuse to stop.

For the healthy runner, real mental toughness is a reality check at the three-quarter mark of a race, when fatigue and oxygen debt cause to you ask, "Why am I here?" Toughness is ignoring the option to slow down or drop out when the bear jumps on your back.

> Good luck with filling each unforgiving minute with sixty seconds worth of distance run.
>
> — With apologies to Coach Rudyard Kipling

APPENDIX

TABLE A: COACH BENSON'S EFFORT-BASED TRAINING CORRELATIONS CHART

Reasons for the 7 Basic Workouts	% of Effort (of Max. O_2 uptake)	=	% Max. HR	Perceived Exertion Feels Like	At min/mile for 20:43 5k runner	Your Pace for Current Fitness	Your Target HR Zone
1. Maintain endurance while getting maximum recovery before a race.	Slogging at 60–65%	=	67–71%	It's too easy, like absolutely no work in being done. It's biomechanically awkward to jog so slowly; it's difficult to even work up a sweat.	9:16 to 8:47	___min/mile	__ to __ BPM
2. Help muscles recover glycogen stores by burning fat as a primary fuel.	Jogging at 65–70%	=	71–75%	It's worth doing; you can at least work up a sweat. You can carry on a full converstaion. It's a fast jog and you are not tired at the end.	8:47 to 8:20	___min/mile	__ to __ BPM
3. Develop local muscle endurance and mental patience.	Running long and easy at 60–75%	=	67–79%	It's a slow run; it's easy to talk. You're rather weary from such a long time on your feet and you might want a nap to recover. Thought you would never get to the end of the workout.	9:16 to 7:57	___min/mile	__ to __ BPM
4. Prepare muscles to make the transition from aerobic to anaerobic running.	Running steadily at 75–80%	=	79–83%	It's a faster pace but still easy enough to sustain "forever." You can still talk in short sentences between gasps; it's your half marathon pace.	7:57 to 7:35	___min/mile	__ to __ BPM
5. Improve anaerobic threshold.	Running hard tempo at 80-85%	=	83-88%	You're running a time trial; you're huffing and puffing too hard to talk. It's uncomfortable for 2–4 miles, but sustainable.	7:35 to 7:15	___min/mile	__ to __ BPM
6. Increase your max. O_2 and improve mental toughness.	Running speedwork at 90–95%	=	92–96%	It's very fast but not all-out. You have enough left to kick the last 100m. It's pain, torture, and agony.	3:23 per 800m to 1:35 per 400m	___min/mile	__ to __ BPM
7. Improve lactic acid tolerance, get very, very tough mentally, and learn to relax as you tie up.	Almost sprinting at 95–100%	=	96–100%	It' significantly faster than race pace. Your legs are full of lead; you are tying up as you near the finish. You are close to full sprint speed. It's over so quick that it fools your HRM.	1:35 per 400m to 39.9 per 200m	___min/mile	__ to __ BPM

Find a printable copy of this chart at www.coachbenson.com/forms

TABLE B: COACH BENSON'S EFFORT-BASED TRAINING PACE AND EFFORT CHART FOR DISTANCE RUNNERS*

Current 5k time is:	Current 10k time is:	60% effort pace per mile	65% effort pace per mile	70% effort pace per mile	75% effort pace per mile	80% effort pace per mile	85% effort pace per mile	90% effort pace per 800m	95% effort pace per 400m	100% effort pace per 200m
13:00 (4:11/mi)	27:00 (4:21/mi)	5:58	5:39	5:22	5:07	4:53	4:40	2:10.8	1:01.7	28.0
13:29 (4:21/mi)	28:00 (4:30/mi)	6:09	5:50	5:33	5:17	5:02	4:49	2:15.0	1:03.6	28.9
13:38 (4:30/mi)	29:00 (4:41/mi)	6:22	6:02	5:44	5:28	5:08	4:59	2:19.8	1:05.9	29.9
14:27 (4:39/mi)	30:00 (4:50/mi)	6:34	6:14	5:55	5:38	5:22	5:09	2:24.0	1:07.9	30:8
14:56 (4:49/mi)	31:00 (5:00/mi)	6:47	6:26	6:07	5:49	5:33	5:19	2:28.8	1:10.1	31.8
15:25 (4:58/mi)	32:00 (5:10/mi)	6:59	6:37	6:17	5:59	5:42	5:28	2:33.0	1:12.1	32.8
15:54 (5:07/mi)	33:00 (5:19/mi)	7:10	6:48	6:27	6:09	5:52	5:37	2:37.2	1:14.1	33.7
16:23 (5:18/mi)	34:00 (5:29/mi)	7:23	7:00	6:39	6:20	6:03	5:47	2:42.0	1:16.3	34.7
16:52 (5:26/mi)	35:00 (5:39/mi)	7:36	7:12	6:51	6:31	6:13	5:57	2:46.8	1:18.6	35.7
17:21 (5:35/mi)	36:00 (5:49/mi)	7:49	7:25	7:02	6:42	6:24	6:07	2:51.4	1:20.8	36.7
17:49 (5:45/mi)	37:00 (5:58/mi)	8:01	7:36	7:13	6:52	6:34	6:16	2:55.8	1:22.8	37.6
18:18 (5:54/mi)	38:00 (6:08/mi)	8:13	7:47	7:23	7:02	6:43	6:25	3:00.0	1:24.8	38.5
18:47 (6:03/mi)	39:00 (6:17/mi)	8:26	7:59	7:35	7:13	6:54	6:36	3:04.6	1:27.0	39.6
19:16 (6:13/mi)	40:00 (6.27/mi)	8:39	8:11	7:47	7:24	7:04	6:46	3:09.4	1:29.2	40.6
19:45 (6:22/mi)	41:00 (6:37/mi)	8:52	8:24	7:58	7:36	7:15	6:56	3:14.1	1:31.5	41.6
20:14 (6:31/mi)	42:00 (6:46/mi)	9:03	8:35	8:09	7:46	7:24	7:05	3:18.4	1:33.5	42.5
20:43 (6:41/mi)	43:00 (6:56/mi)	9:16	8:47	8:20	7:57	7:35	7:15	3:23.2	1:35.7	43.5
21:11 (6:50/mi)	44:00 (7:06/mi)	9:28	8:58	8:31	8:07	7:44	7:24	3:27.4	1:37.7	44.4
21:41 (6:59/mi)	45:00 (7:16/mi)	9:41	9:10	8:43	8:18	7:55	7:34	3:32.2	1:39.9	45.4
22:10 (7:09/mi)	46:00 (7:25 mi)	9:52	9:21	8:53	8:28	8:05	7:43	3:36.4	1:41.9	46.3
22:38 (7:18/mi)	47:00 (7:35/mi)	10:04	9:32	9:03	8:37	8:14	7:52	3:40.6	1:43.9	47.2
23:07 (7:27 mi)	48:00 (7:44/mi)	10:17	9:44	9:15	8:49	8:25	8:03	3:45.4	1:46.2	48.3
23:46 (7:37/mi)	49:00 (7:54/mi)	10:28	9:55	9:25	8:59	8:34	8:12	3:49.6	1:48.1	49.2
24:05 (7:46/mi)	50:00 (8:04/mi)	10:41	10:08	9:37	9:10	8:45	8:22	3:54.2	1:50.4	50.2
24:34 (7:55/mi)	51:00 (8:14/mi)	10:53	10:18	9:48	9:20	8:54	8:31	3:58.4	1:52.4	51.1
25:03 (8:05/mi)	52:00 (8:23/mi)	11:06	10:31	9:59	9:31	9:05	8:41	4:03.2	1:54.6	52.1
25:32 (8:14/mi)	53:00 (8:33/mi)	11:17	10:42	10:10	9:41	9:14	8:50	4:07.4	1:56.6	53.0
26:01 (8:24/mi)	54:00 (8:43/mi)	11:29	10:53	10:20	9:51	9:24	8:59	4:11.6	1:58.6	53.9
26:30 (8:33/mi)	55:00 (8:52/mi)	11:42	11:05	10:32	10:02	9:34	9:09	4:16.4	2:00.8	54.9
26:59 (8:42/mi)	56:00 (9:02/mi)	11:54	11:16	10:42	10:12	9:44	9:17	4:20.6	2:02.8	55.8
27:28 (8:51/mi)	57:00 (9:11/mi)	12:05	11:27	10:53	10:21	9:53	9:27	4:24.8	2:04.8	56.7
27:56 (9:01/mi)	58:00 (9:21/mi)	12:18	11:39	11:04	10:33	10:04	9:38	4:29.6	2:07.0	57.7
28:25 (9:10/mi)	59:00 (9:31/mi)	12:29	11:50	11:15	10:43	10:13	9:47	4:33.8	2:09.0	58.6
28:54 (9:19/mi)	60:00 (9:41/mi)	12:41	12:01	11:25	10:52	10:23	9:56	4:38.0	2:11.0	59.5

*Note: Paces listed for 95%, and especially 100%, should be done by pace and not heart rate.

Find a printable copy of this chart at www.coachbenson.com/forms

TABLE C: TARGET HEART RATE CALCULATOR

HOW TO USE THIS CHART

Locate you Resting Heart Rate (RHR) on the left-hand axis of this nomogram. Next, locate your Maximum Heart Rate (MHR) on the inside of the far right-hand axis. If you do not know your MHR, use your age on the outside of the right-hand axis to estimate it. Finally, draw a straight line from your RHR to your MHR. Where the line intersects the scale of your targeted intensity represents the corresponding predicted heart rate that you should average in order to achieve your planned level of effort.

The graph is based on the Karvonen formula. The formula used for correlating MHR to age is:

MHR = 208 – (0.7 × age)

Find a printable copy of this form at www.coachbenson.com/forms

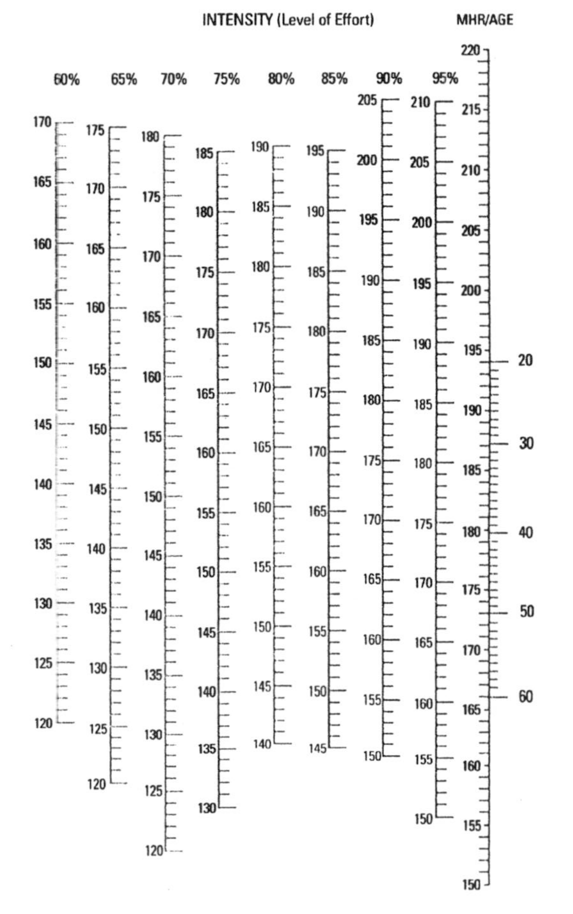

TABLE D

TRAINING PLAN AND RACE SCHEDULE FOR:________

Week Date	Phase				Miles/ Week	Days/ Week	Mileage Per Day							Race Schedule/Special Notes
	I	II	III	IV			M	T	W	TH	F	S	SU	

GOALS AND OBJECTIVES:

Find a printable copy of this chart at www.coachbenson.com/forms

TABLE E: SAMPLE PLAN FOR H.S.RUNNER'S 5K CROSS-COUNTRY SEASON AND ADULT ROAD RUNNER'S 5K

Find a printable copy of this plan at www.coachbenson.com/forms

TRAINING PLAN AND RACE SCHEDULE FOR: *Favorite Reader*

Week Date	Phase				Miles/ Week	Days/ Week	Mileage Per Day							Race Schedule/Special Notes
	I	II	III	IV			M	T	W	TH	F	S	SU	
1-Jul	xx				25	5							LR 5	LR = Long runs on Sundays
8-Jul	xx				29	5							5	
23-Dec	xx				35	5							6	
22-Jul	xx				39	6							7	
29-Jul	xx				46	6							9	
5-Aug	xx				35	6							7	
12-Aug	xx				53	6							11	
19-Aug	xx				60	7							14	
26-Aug	xx				55	6							10	
2-Sep	xx				45	6						5k	11	Time trail or race to establish fitness level
9-Sep		xx			50	6						5k	12	Cross-country
16-Sep		xx			40	6						5k	10	Cross-bountry or 5k road race
23-Sep		xx			45	5							8	
30-Sep		xx			40	5						5k	10	Cross-country or road race
7-Oct		xx			40	6						race	8	5k or cross-bountry or 10k road race
14-Oct		xx			40	5						race	6	5k cross-country
21-Oct			xx		35	6							10	
28-Oct			xx		30	6						5k	7	Cross-country or road race
4-Nov			xx		35	6							10	
11-Nov			xx		40	6						5k	7	Cross-country or road race
18-Nov				xx	25	5							6	
25-Nov				xx	20	6						5k	6	Cross-country or road race
2-Dec				xx	20	6						5k	6	Peak performance race for PRs

GOALS AND OBJECTIVES: Break 17:49 for 5,000m cross-country or road race

TABLE F

WEEKLY TRAINING PATTERN FOR:

Favorite Reader ____________

PHASE: __

FROM: ______ *to* _____

EASY DAYS:

Mon. ❑ Tues. ❑ Wed. ❑ Thurs. ❑ Fri. ❑ Sat. ❑ Sun. ❑

MILEAGE: Run anywhere from _ to _ miles per day, according to plan, at ___% to ___% effort. Your target heart rate range will be
____ up to ____ bpm.

These are slower runs for building either ENDURANCE and or RECOVERING from speedwork and races. Relax and enjoy them. Consider taking off one or two of these days or, if you must, jog easy within the mileage guidelines given above. This is also a good day for cross-training instead of running.

After running, stretch and run _ to _ strides for _ to _ seconds. These fast but easy runs will help to rebalance the biomechanics of your stride. Slow runs are bad for you, if they are all you run.

HARD DAYS:

A: INTERVALS

Mon. ❑ Tues. ❑ Wed. ❑ Thurs. ❑ Fri. ❑ Sat. ❑ Sun. ❑

These are "speed" workouts for maintaining leg strength, flexibility and coordination.

First jog one to two miles stretch and run five strides for 15

Run __ to __ X ____ in _ at __% to __% effort with a __ meter jog recovery interval. Your THR will be ___ to ___ at the end of each repeat, and should be down to ____% by the end of the interval of recovery jog. Finish the workout with _ sets of drills over ___ meters. (High Knees, Fanny Flickers, Skip Bounding, and Toe Walk.)

B: Hard and Hilly Heart Rate Fartleks

Mon. ❑ Tues. ❑ Wed. ❑ Thurs. ❑ Fri. ❑ Sat. ❑ Sun. ❑

MILEAGE: Run _ to _ total miles and include _ to _* minutes of Hard and Hilly Heart Rate Fartleks at __% to __% effort. Your target heart rate will range from ___ up to ___ bmp.

After running, stretch.

***Total 8–12 minutes of uphill running on several hills with 80% effort as max. Recover between hills with jogging until heart rate is 70%.**

Steady-state and Anaerobic Threshold Days:

Mon. ❑ Tues. ❑ Wed. ❑ Thurs. ❑ Fri. ❑ Sat. ❑ Sun. ❑

These workouts are exquisitely tailored to build up your stamina without tearing you down the slightest bit. They are in the immortal words of my high school biology teacher, Fred Cook, anabolic, not catabolic. You can look it up. And while you're at it, note very well that these workouts are a far cry from real interval workouts, so don't worry if they seem easier than you are used to doing. Just enjoy not having to bust it for a change. Start both the below workouts with a mile or two of easy warm-up running and then, boogie on down.

A: If You Are in Phase I or Marathon Training:

MILEAGE: Run anywhere from ___ to ___ steady-state miles, according to plan, at ___% to ___% effort. Your target heart rate range will be from _____ up to _____ bpm and your pace should be ____ to ____ mpm.

B: If You Are in Phases II, III, or IV:

MILEAGE: Run anywhere from ____ to ____ miles, according to plan, and include ____ to ____ miles/minutes at ___% to ___% effort. Your target heart rate range will be from _____ up to _____ bpm and your pace should be _____ to ____ mpm.

Jog at least one minute to cool down and stretch.

4. Long Runs:

Mon. ❑ Tues. ❑ Wed. ❑ Thurs. ❑ Fri. ❑ Sat. ❑ Sun. ❑

These workouts have two purposes: to build endurance during Phase I and then to maintain it during the other phases. Thus, note well the changes in your THR when you switch phases.

MILEAGE: Run from ___ to ___ miles, according to plan, at ___% to ___% effort. Your target heart rate range will be from ____ up to ____ bpm and your pace should be ___ to ___ mpm.

Be sure to stretch really well and do four or five 15-second strides to get the kinks out and to rebalance your prime mover muscles.

Happy trails!

TABLE G1: COACH BENSON'S EFFORT-BASED TRAINING PACE AND EFFORT CHART FOR MIDDLE-DISTANCE RUNNERS

Current 800m time is:	Current mile time is:	Current 2 mile time is:	Current 5k time is:	60% effort pace per mile	65% effort pace per mile	70% effort pace per mile	75% effort pace per mile	80% effort pace per mile	85% effort pace per mile	90% effort pace per 800m	95% effort pace per 400m
1:42	3:45	8:02 (4:01/mi)	13:00 (4:11/mi)	15:58	5:39	5:22	5:07	4:53	4:40	2:10.8	1:01.9
1:46	3:54	8:20 (4:10/mi)	13:29 (4:21/mi)	6:09	5:50	5:33	5:17	5:02	4:49	2:15.0	1:03.6
1:49	4:02	8:37 (4:18/mi)	13:58 (4:30/mi)	6:22	6:02	5:44	5:28	5:12	4:59	2:19.8	1:05.9
1:53	4:11	8:57 (4:28/mi)	14:27 (4:39/mi)	6:34	6:14	5:55	5:38	5:22	5:09	2:24.0	1:07.9
1:58	4:20	9:18 (4:39/mi)	14:56 (4:49/mi)	6:47	6:26	6:07	5:49	5:33	5:19	2:28.8	1:10.1
2:01	4:28	9:34 (4:47/mi)	15:25 (4:58/mi)	6:59	6:37	6:17	5:59	5:42	5:28	2:33.0	1:12.1
2:05	4:37	9:53 (4:56/mi)	15:54 (5:07/mi)	7:10	6:48	6:27	6:09	5:52	5:37	2:37.2	1:14.1
2:09	4:46	10:12 (5:06/mi)	16:23 (5:18/mi)	7:23	7:00	6:39	6:20	6:03	5:47	2:42.0	1:16.3
2:13	4:54	10:29 (5:14/mi)	16:52 (5:26/mi)	7:36	7:12	6:51	6:31	6:13	5:57	2:46.8	1:18.6
2:17	5:03	10:49 (5:24/mi)	17:21 (5:35/mi)	7:49	7:25	7:02	6:42	6:24	6:07	2:51.4	1:20.8
2:21	5:12	11:08 (5:34/mi)	17:49 (5:45/mi)	8:01	7:36	7:13	6:52	6:34	6:16	2:55.8	1:22.8
2:25	5:21	11:28 (5:44/mi	18:18 (5:54/mi)	8:13	7:47	7:23	7:02	6:43	6:25	3:00.0	1:24.8
2:29	5:29	11:43 (5:51/mi)	18:47 (6:03/mi)	8:26	7:59	7:35	7:13	6:54	6:36	3:04.6	1:27.0
2:33	5:38	12:02 (6:02/mi)	19:16 (6:13/mi)	8:39	8:11	7:47	7:24	7:04	6:46	3:09.4	1:29.2
2:37	5:47	12:22 (6:11/mi)	19:45 (6:22/mi)	8:52	8:24	7:58	7:36	7:15	6:56	3:14.1	1:31.5
2:41	5:56	12:41 (6:20/mi)	20:14 (6:31/mi)	9:03	8:35	8:09	7:46	7:24	7:05	3:18.4	1:33.5
2:44	6:04	12:57 (6:28/mi)	20:43 (6:41/mi)	9:16	8:47	8:20	7:57	7:35	7:15	3:23.2	1:35.7
2:48	6:13	13:16 (6:38/mi)	21:11 (6:50/mi)	9:28	8:58	8:31	8:07	7:44	7:24	3:27.4	1:37.7
2:53	6:22	13:34 (6:47/mi	21:41 (6:59/mi)	9:41	9:10	8:43	8:18	7:55	7:34	3:32.2	1:39.9
2:57	6:31	13:54 (6:57/mi)	22:10 (7:09/mi)	9:52	9:21	8:53	8:28	8:05	7:43	3:36.4	1:41.9
3:00	6:39	14:09 (7:04/mi)	22:38 (7:18/mi)	10:02	9:32	9:03	8:37	8:14	7:52	3:40.6	1:43.9
3:04	6:48	14:29 (7:14/mi)	23:07 (7:27/mi)	10:17	9:44	9:15	8:49	8:25	8:03	3:45.4	1:46.2
3:08	6:57	14:47 (7:23/mi)	23:46 (7:39/mi)	10:28	9:55	9:25	8:59	8:34	8:12	3:49.6	1:48.1

Train Smart Paces explained (Assumes a highly fit runner in a competivive phase of training).
70% effort pace and below is considered an easy aerobic effort.
75% to 80% effort pace is considered a moderately hard effort.
85% effort is a pace that is sustainable for just over 1 hour under racing conditions.
90% effort is a pace that is sustainable for exacly 30 minutes under racing conditions.
95% effort is a pace that is sustainable for exactly 11 minutes under racing conditions.

Sample workouts:
Run 6 to 8 miles below 70% effort for an easy aerobic effort. (Suitable for any phase of training.)

Run 3 to 4 times a mile at 85% effort with a 400-meter recovery jog between each repeat to increase strength as well as aerobic capacity. (Suitable for a runner in phase II, III or IV of training.)

Run 6 to 8 times 800 meters at 90% effort with a 400-meter recovery jog between each repeat to increase strength as well as aerobic capacity. (Suitable for a runner in phase III or IV of training.)

Run 10 to 12 times 400 meters at 95% effort with a 200-meter recovery jog between each repeat to produce maximum gains in your aerobic capacity. (Suitable for a runner in phase III or IV of training.)

TABLE G2: COACH BENSON'S EFFORT-BASED TRAINING PACE AND EFFORT CHART FOR MIDDLE-DISTANCE RUNNERS

Current 800m time is:	Current mile time is:	Current 2 mile time is:	Current 5k time is:	800 meter specialists 100% effort pace per			1 mile specialists 100% effort pace per		
				100m	200m	300m	200m	300m	400m
1:42	3:45	8:02 (4:01/mi)	13:00 (4:11/mi)	12.1	24.3	36.4	25.7	38.5	51.4
1:46	3:54	8:20 (4:10/mi)	13:29 (4:21/mi)	12.5	24.9	37.4	26.5	39.7	53.0
1:49	4:02	8:37 (4:18/mi)	13:58 (4:30/mi)	12.9	25.8	38.8	27.4	41.1	54.9
1:53	4:11	8:57 (4:28/mi)	14:27 (4:39/mi)	13.3	26.6	39.9	28.3	42.5	56.7
1:58	4:20	9:18 (4:39/mi)	14:56 (4:49/mi)	13.7	27.5		29.2	43.8	58.4
2:01	4:28	9:34 (4:47/mi)	15:25 (4:58/mi)	14.1	28.3		30.0	45.0	60.0
2:05	4:37	9:53 (4:56/mi)	15:54 (5:07/mi)	14.5	29.1		30.9	46.3	
2:09	4:46	10:12 (5:06/mi)	16:23 (5:18/mi)	15.0	29.9		31.8	47.7	
2:13	4:54	10:29 (5:14/mi)	16:52 (5:26/mi)	15.4	30.8		32.7	49.0	
2:17	5:03	10:49 (5:24/mi)	17:21 (5:35/mi)	15.8	31.7		33.7	50.5	
2:21	5:12	11:08 (5:34/mi)	17:49 (5:45/mi)	16.2	32.5		34.5	51.7	
2:25	5:21	11:28 (5:44/mi)	18:18 (5:54/mi)	16.6	33.3		35.3	52.9	
2:29	5:29	11:43 (5:51/mi)	18:47 (6:03/mi)	17.1	34.1		36.3	54.4	
2:33	5:38	12:02 (6:01/mi)	19.16 (6:13/mi)	17.5	35.0		37.2	55.8	
2:37	5:47	12:22 (6:11/mi)	19:45 (6:22/mi)	17.9	35.9		38.1	57.1	
2:41	5:56	12:41 (6:20/mi)	20:14 (6:31/mi)	18.3	36.7		39.0	58.5	
2:44	6:04	12:57 (6:28/mi)	20:43 (6:41/mi)	18.8	37.5		39.9	59.8	
2:48	6:13	13:16 (6:38/mi)	21:11 (6:50/mi)	19.2	38.3		40.7		
2:53	6:22	13:34 (6:47/mi)	21:41 (6:59/mi)	19.6	39.2		41.6		
2:57	6:31	13:54 (6:57/mi)	22:10 (7:09/mi)	20.0	40.0		42.5		
3:00	6:39	14:09 (7:04/mi)	22:38 (7:18/mi)	20.4			43.3		
3:04	6:48	14:29 (7:14/mi)	23:07 (7:27/mi)	20.8			44.2		
3:08	6:57	14:47 (7:23/mi)	23:46 (7:37/mi)	21.2			45.0		

Train Smart Paces explained: (Assumes a highly fit runner in a competitive phase of training.)

800 meter speecialists should not run longer than 40 seconds at the specified paces.
1 mile specialists should not run longer than 1 minute at the specificed paces.
2 miles specialists should not run longer than 1 minute and 30 seconds at the specified paces.
5k specialists should not run longer than 2 minutes at the specified paces.
As a result, the 200, 300, and 400 meter paces are not listed beyond the time limits for your current fitness level.

Sample workouts: (Phases 3 and 4 of training)

An 800 meter or a 1 mile specialist might run 10 to 12 times 200 meters with full recoveries between 200 meters, to as much as 400 meters between each repetition.
A 2 mile speciaist might run 10 to 12 times 300 meters, with 300 meter recoveries between each repetition.
A 5k specialist might run 10 to 12 times 400 meters, with 400 meter recovereies between each repetition. (A printable copy of this chart is available at www.coachbenson.com/forms.)

TABLE G3: COACH BENSON'S EFFORT-BASED TRAINING PACE AND EFFORT CHART FOR MIDDLE-DISTANCE RUNNERS

Current 800m time is:	Current mile time is:	Current 2 mile time is:	Current 5k time is:	2 mile specialists 100% effort pace per 200m	300m	400m	5k specialists 100% effort pace per 200m	300m	400m
1:42	3:45	8:02 (4:01/mi)	13:00 (4:11/mi)	26.8	40.2	53.6	28.0	42.0	56.0
1:46	3:54	8:20 (4:10/mi)	13:29 (4:21/mi)	27.6	41.4	55.3	28.9	43.3	57.8
1:49	4:02	8:37 (4:18/mi)	13:58 (4:30/mi)	28.6	42.9	57.3	29.9	44.8	59.8
1:53	4:11	8:57 (4:28/mi)	14:27 (4:39/mi)	29.5	44.7	59.0	30.8	46.2	1:01.6
1:58	4:20	9:18 (4:39/mi)	14:56 (4:49/mi)	30.5	45.7	1:01.0	31.8	47.7	1:03.6
2:01	4:28	9:34 (4:47/mi)	15:25 (4:58/mi)	31.3	46.5	1:02.7	32.8	49.2	1:05.5
2:05	4:37	9:53 (4:56/mi)	15:54 (5:07/mi)	32.2	48.3	1:04.4	33.7	50.5	1:07.3
2:09	4:46	10:12 (5:06/mi)	16:23 (5:18/mi)	33.2	49.8	1:06.4	34.7	52.0	1:09.4
2:13	4:54	10:29 (5:14/mi)	16:52 (5:26/mi)	34.2	51.2	1:08.3	35.7	5.35	1:14.4
2:17	5:03	10:49 (5:24/mi)	17:21 (5:35/mi)	35.1	52.6	1:10.3	36.7	55.0	1:34.4
2:21	5:12	11:08 (5:34/mi)	17:49 (5:45/mi)	36.0	54.0	1:12.0	37.6	56.4	1:15.3
2:25	5:21	11:28 (5:44/mi)	18:18 (5:54/mi)	36.9	55.3	1:03.7	38.5	57.7	1:17.1
2:29	5:29	11:43 (5:51/mi)	18:47 (6:03/mi)	37.8	56.7	1:15.7	39.6	59.4	1:19.1
2:33	5:38	12:02 (6:01/mi)	19.16 (6:13/mi)	38.8	58.2	1:17.6	40.6	1:00.9	1:21.1
2:37	5:47	12:22 (6:11/mi)	19:45 (6:22/mi)	39.8	59.7	1:19.6	41.6	102.4	1:23.2
2:41	5:56	12:41 (6:20/mi)	20:14 (6:31/mi)	40.6	1:00.9	1:21.3	42.5	1:03.7	1:25.0
2:44	6:04	12:57 (6:28/mi)	20:43 (6:41/mi)	41.6	1:02.4	1:23.2	43.5	1:05.2	1:27.0
2:48	6:13	13:16 (6:38/mi)	21:11 (6:50/mi)	42.5	10:3.7	1:25.0	44.4	1:06.6	1:28.8
2:53	6:22	13:34 (6:47/mi)	21:41 (6:59/mi)	43.5	1:05.2	1:26.9	45.4	1:08.1	1:30.9
2:57	6:31	13:54 (6:57/mi)	22:10 (7:09/mi)	44.3	1:06.4	1:28.6	46.3	1:09.5	1:32.7
3:00	6:39	14:09 (7:04/mi)	22:38 (7:18/mi)	45.1	1:07.7		47.2	1:10.8	1:34.4
3:04	6:48	14:29 (7:14/mi)	23:07 (7:27/mi)	46.1	1:09.2		48.2	1:12.4	1:36.5
3:08	6:57	14:47 (7:23/mi)	23:46 (7:37/mi)	47.0	1:10.5		49.1	1:13.7	1:38.2

Train Smart paces explained: (Assumes a highly fit runner in a competitive phase of training.)

800 meter speecialists should not run longer than 40 seconds at the specified paces.
1 mile specialists should not run longer than 1 minute at the specificed paces.
2 miles specialists should not run longer than 1 minute and 30 seconds at the specified paces.
5k specialists should not run longer than 2 minutes at the specified paces.
As a result, the 200, 300, and 400 meter paces are not listed beyond the time limits for your current fitness level.

Sample workouts: (Phases 3 and 4 of training)

An 800 meter or a 1 mile specialist might run 10 to 12 times 200 meters with full recoveries between 200 meters, to as much as 400 meters between each repetition.
A 2 mile speciaist might run 10 to 12 times 300 meters, with 300 meter recoveries between each repetition.
A 5k specialist might run 10 to 12 times 400 meters, with 400 meter recoveries between each repetition. (A printable copy of this chart is available at www.coachbenson.com/forms.)

TABLE H1: COACH BENSON'S EFFORT-BASED TRAINING — 80/90 WORKOUTS FOR MARATHON RUNNERS

Your current 10k time is:	Your realistic marathon prediced time is:	Your ideal marathon predicted time is:	Your realistic 80%* effort pace per mile is:	Your ideal 80% effort pace per mile is:	Your realistic 90% effort pace per 880 yds. is:	Your ideal 90%** effort pace per 880 yds. is:
27:00 (4:21/mi)	2:09:02 (4:55/mi)	2:04:31 (4:45/mi)	5:02	4:53	2:20.8	2:05.6
28:00 (4:30/mi)	2:13:47 (5:06/mi)	2:09:02 (5:17/mi)	5:12	5:02	2:15.0	2:10.8
29:00 (4:41/mi)	2:18;29 (5:17/mi)	2:13;47 (5:06/mi)	5:22	5:12	2:19.8	2:15.0
30:00 (4:50/mi)	2:23;10 (5:27/mi)	2:18;29 (5:17/mi)	5:33	5:22	2:24.0	2:19.8
31:00 (5:00mi)	2:27;50 (5:38/mi)	2:23;10 (5:27/mi)	5:42	5:33	2:28.8	2:24.0
32:00 (5:10/mi)	2:32;35 (5:49/mi)	2:27;50 (5:38/mi)	5:52	5:42	2:33.0	2:28.8
33:00 (5:19/mi)	2:37;10 (5:59/mi)	2:32;35 (5:49/mi)	6:03	5:53	2:37.2	2:33.0
34:00 (5:29/mi)	2:41;44 (6:10/mi)	2:37;10 (5:59/mi)	6:13	6:03	2:43.0	2:37.2
35:00 (5:39/mi)	2:46;23 (6:21/mi)	2:41;44 (6:10/mi)	6:24	6:13	2:46.8	2:42.0
36:00 (5:49/mi)	2:51;00 (6:31/mi)	2:46;23 (6:21/mi)	6:34	6:24	2:51.4	2:46.8
37:00 (5:58/mi)	2:55;33 (6:42/mi)	2:51;00 (6:31/mi)	6:43	6:34	2:55.8	2:51.4
38:00 (6:08/mi)	3:00;15 (6:52/mi)	2:55;33 (6:42/mi)	6:54	6:43	3:00.0	2:55.8
39:00 (6:17/mi)	3:04;41 (7:02/mi)	3:00;15 (6:52/mi)	7:04	6:54	3:04.6	3:00.0
40:00 (6:27/mi)	3:09;14 (7:13/mi)	3:04;41 (7:02/mi)	7:15	7:04	3:09.4	3:04.6
41:00 (6:37/mi)	3:13;48 (7:23/mi)	3:09;14 (7:13/mi)	7:24	7:15	3:14.1	3:09.4
42:00 (6:46/mi)	3:18;14 (7:34/mi)	3:13;48 (7:23/mi)	7:35	7:24	3:18.4	3:14.1
43:00 (6:56/mi)	3:22;50 (7:44/mi)	3:18;14 (7:34/mi)	7:44	7:35	3:23.2	3:18.4
44:00 (7:06/mi)	3:27;15 (7:54/mi)	3:22;50 (7:44/mi)	7:55	7:44	3:27.4	3:23.2
45:00 (7:16/mi)	3:31;43 (8:04/mi)	3:27;15 (7:54/mi)	8:05	7:55	3:32.2	3:27.4
46:00 (7:25/mi)	3:36;12 (8:15/mi)	3:31;43 (8:04/mi)	8:14	8:05	3:36.4	3:32.2
47:00 (7:35/mi)	3:40;39 (8:25/mi)	3:36;12 (8:15/mi)	8:25	8:14	3:40.6	3:36.4
48:00 (7:44/mi)	3:45;04 (8:35/mi)	3:40;39 (8:25/mi)	8:34	8:25	3:45.4	3:40.6
49:00 (7:54/mi)	3:49;31 (8:45/mi)	3:45;04 (8:35/mi)	8:45	8:34	3:49.6	3:45.4
50:00 (8:04/mi)	3:53;52 (8:54/mi)	3:49;31 (8:45/mi)	8:54	8:45	3:54.2	3:49.6
51:00 (8:14/mi)	3:58;24 (9:05/mi)	3:53;52 (8:54/mi)	9:05	8:54	3:58.4	3:54.2
52:00 (8:23/mi)	4:02;42 (9:15/mi)	3:58;24 (9:05/mi)	9:14			
9:054:03.2	3:58.4					

(Continued on next page.)

Your current 10k time is:	Your realistic marathon prediced time is:	Your ideal marathon predicted time is:	Your realistic 80%* effort pace per mile is:	Your ideal 80% effort pace per mile is:	Your realistic 90% effort pace per 880m is:	Your ideal 90%** effort pace per 880m is:
53:00 (8:33/mi)	4:07.06 (9:25/mi)	4:02.42 (9:15/mi)	9:24	9:14	4:07.4	4:03.2
54:00 (8:43/mi)	4:11.28 (9:35/mi)	4:07.06 (9:25/mi)	9:34	9:24	4:11.6	4:07.4
55:00 (8:52/mi)	4:15.50 (9:45/mi)	4:11.28 (9:35/mi)	9:44	9:34	4:16.4	4:11.6
56:00 (9:02/mi)	4:20.10 (9:55/mi)	4:15.50 (9:45/mi)	9:53	9:44	4:20.6	4:16.4
57:00 (9:11/mi)	4:24.30 (10:05/mi)	4:20.10 (9:55/mi)	10:04	9:53	4:24.8	4:20.6
58:00 (9:21/mi)	4:28.48 (10:15/mi)	4:24.30 (10:05/mi)	10:13	10:04	4:29.6	4:24.8
59:00 (9:31/mi)	4:33.07 (10:25/mi)	4:28.48 (10:15/mi)	10:23	10:13	4:33.8	4:29.6
60:00 (9:41/mi)	4:37.05 (10:34/mi)	4:33.07 (10:25/mi)	10:33	10:23	4:38.0	4:33.8

Keys to success: (And the proper way to use this chart.)

Chose your marathon pace based on your current 10k time as well as your knowledge as to the type of runner you are, a pure marathoner, or a short distance specialist. Pure marathoners would use the ideal 80% paces listed, while short distance specialists, would use the realistic *80% pace, which in reality is more like 77% to 78% effort. If wearing a heart monitor, do not exceed a heart rate greater than 80% of your training range. Except for elite runners, who can on occasion exceed 80% effort due to the shorter duraction of their marathon, 80% effort pace/heart rate is usually within on or two seconds per mile of your marathon pace. Keep in mind though, not all runners can maintain an 80% effort for the entire marathon. As they say, "Choose your parents wisely."

Run your 880 yard repeats in the ranges given for your current fitness level. The paces are given in minutes and seconds, but are very near your predicted marathon time in hours and minutes. Never exceed 90% effort for your 880s. If you feel the need to make the workout more difficult, run the recoveries faster. Also, your recovery jogs of ¼ mile should take no longer than the time it took you to run your 880s, while still allowing you to recover to a minimum of 70% effort.

Sample Workouts:

Marathon pace runs: Run 8 to 13 miles at your predicted pace based on your current 10k times, not exceeding 80% effort.

Track workouts: Run 6 to 10 times 880 yards at no more than 90% effort, with a recovery jog between each repeat, recovering to at least 70% effort.

Note:

**The ideal 90% effort pace is somewhat faster than a true 90% effort. With proper training, this more aggressive pace should be attainable by individuals ready to make the jump to the next level, making their ideal marathon pace also more attainable.

A printable copy of this chart is availalbe at www.coachbeson.com/forms.

TABLE I

TRAINING PLAN AND RACE SCHEDULE FOR: *Favorite Marathoner*

Week Date	Phase				Miles/ Week	Days/ Week	Mileage Per Day							Race Schedule/Special Notes
	I	II	III	IV			M	T	W	TH	F	S	SU	
9-Dec		X												Sunday: Long runs
16-Dec		X			30–35	5–6							10–11	
23-Dec		X			30–35	5–6							10–11	
30-Dec		X			30–35	5–6							10–11	
6-Jan			M		38	5–6		A4			C4		12	
13-Jan			A		42	6		B3			C4		14	
20-Jan			R		37	5		A4			D6		12	
27-Jan			A		45	6		B3			C6		16	
3-Feb			T		40	5–6		A6			D8		13	
10-Feb			H		45–50	6–7		B4			C7		18–20	
17-Feb			O	T	38–42	5–6		A8			D8		13	
24-Feb			N	R	49–54	7		B4			C8		20–21	
3-Mar				A	40–44	6		A10			D10		13	
10-Mar				I	52–58	7		B5			C8		21–22	
17-Mar				N	40–45	6		A12			D12		13	
24-Mar				I	55–60	7		B6			C8		22–23	
31-Mar				N	40–45	6		A8			D8		10	
7-Apr				G	21	7	3	5	3	3	2	3	2	Cross-country or road race
14-Apr							26.2							BAA Marathon

A = # × 880 at <90% in 3:30 with 440 yard jog at 70%.
B = # × miles at goal pace minus 30 seconds with 2:00 jog.
C = # × 60–90 second uphill repeats at 85–90% jog down with recovery to 65%.
D = # of miles of Planned Marathon Pace runs at 80%.

GOALS AND OBJECTIVES: FINISH BOSTON MARATHON IN 3:20 OR BETTER

FURTHER READING

Bailey, Covert and Lea Bishop. *The Complete Fit or Fat Book.* New York: Galahad Books, 2001.

Bannister, Roger and Frederick C. Klein. *The Four-minute Mile.* Guilford, Conn.: The Lyons Press, 1994.

Daniels, Jack and Alberto Salazar. *Daniels' Running Formula.* Champaign, Ill.: Human Kinetics, 1998.

Martin, David E. and Peter N. Coe (contributor). *Better Training for Distance Runners.* Champaign, Ill.: Human Kinetics, 1997.

Noakes, Timothy. *Lore of Running,* 4th edition. Champaign, Ill.: Human Kinetics, 2002.

Sandrock, Michael. *Running with the Legends: with the Training and Racing Insights from 21 Great Runners.* Champaign, Ill.: Human Kinetics, 1996.

ABOUT THE AUTHOR

Roy T. Benson, MPE, C.F.I., is an exercise scientist and distance running coach. He has a B.A. degree from Dartmouth College and a master's degree in physical education with an emphasis in exercise physiology from the University of Florida. Since 1976, he has held a national certification as a fitness instructor from the American College of Sports Medicine. He has presented over 400 professional papers and lectures for academic and general audiences.

Benson currently serves as a senior writer for *Running Times* and contributing editor for *Running Journal* magazines. He is also a contributing writer for *Peak Running Performance* newsletter. Combined readership is over 200,000 runners. His booklet *Precision Running,* published by Polar Electro of Finland, has sold well over 150,000 copies and has been translated into seven languages. *The Runner's Coach,* Benson's book on effort-based training, is in its second printing. His computerized training program, *Coach Benson's Heart Rate Training,* has been a best-selling program from PC Coach/Biometrics, Inc. of Boulder, Colorado.

Coach Benson ran competitively for over forty years with personal bests of 1:53.4 for 880 yards and 4:19.8 for the mile. As a masters runner, Benson has run 36:06 for 10k, 17:22 for 5k, 4:52 for the mile, and has qualified for the Boston marathon with a 3:09.05 PR.

He has coached professionally for 40 years for military, club, university, and high school teams. From 1969-79, at the University of Florida, Benson served as head cross-country coach for seven years and head track coach for three years. During his tenure with the Gators, he was the president, then executive director of the world-famous Florida Track Club that placed marathon gold medalist Frank Shorter and ninth place finisher Jack Bachelor on the 1972 U.S. Olympic team. Coach Benson was a national advisory coach to the Philippine Olympic track team that competed in the 1972 Munich Olympics.

Since 1993, Coach Benson has been a part-time community coach for Marist School in Atlanta. His boys and girls teams have won seven state AAAA cross-country championships. Through the 2002 season, the girls have won five straight team championships with Christy Brewer becoming the seventeenth Marist runner to win individual state track and cross-country titles. His most successful female athlete, Kyla Barbour, placed sixteenth and then seventh at the national Foot Locker Cross-Country Championships in her junior and senior years. 1999 graduate Brendon Mahoney was two-time state cross-country champion and was undefeated in the mile his senior year, winning the National Scholastic Championship Meet in 4:04.78. In that race, he defeated Allan Webb and pulled him to the 4:06 that broke Jim Ryun's sophomore year national record. Mahoney also ran 1:49.8 for 800 meters after breaking a 23 year-old state record while winning the state championship in 1:50.1.

Benson is currently the owner and president of Running, Ltd., a company in Atlanta that has been operating Nike-sponsored summer camps for both adult and high school runners in North Carolina and Vermont for the past thirty-one years. The camps involve over 1,200 runners and coaches annually. In between summers, Benson offers private coaching services to adult roadrunners in the United States, Europe, and South America. He is a consultant for NIKE [techlab™ helping design, develop and promote their pace, distance, and heart rate monitors.